CONFEDERATION OF THE BRITISH WEST INDIES

versus

ANNEXATION TO THE UNITED STATES OF AMERICA

CONFEDERATION OF THE BRITISH WEST INDIES

versus

ANNEXATION TO THE UNITED STATES OF AMERICA

A POLITICAL DISCOURSE ON THE WEST INDIES

BY

LOUIS S. MEIKLE, M.D., D.D.S.

BORN NOV. 24, 1874, MANCHESTER, JAMAICA, B.W.I.

*Graduate of the Medical and Dental Colleges, Howard University, Wash.
D.C., U.S.A.; Late Demonstrator of Dentistry, Dental College, Howard
University; Late Asst. Surgeon St. Pythias Sanatorium, Hot Springs,
Arkansas, U.S.A.; Late Medical Inspector Isthmian Canal Commission,
Canal Zone, Republic of Panama; Late (Lieutenant) Asst. Surgeon,
Colon Fire Brigade, Colon, Republic of Panama; Late Secretary
Citizens' League, Colon, Republic of Panama; Inventor
Firemen's Equipment, Patent No. 932,880, U.S.A. Patent
Office; Inventor Sectional Dirigible Airship—see British
Admiralty Office*

NEGRO UNIVERSITIES PRESS
NEW YORK

Originally published in 1912
by Sampson Low, Marston & Company, Ltd.

Reprinted from a copy in the collections
of the Brooklyn Public Library

Reprinted 1969 by
Negro Universities Press
A DIVISION OF GREENWOOD PRESS, INC.
NEW YORK

SBN 8371-2728-9

PRINTED IN UNITED STATES OF AMERICA

TO MY FRIEND

WALTER HAMBLE CARRINGTON, Esq., B.A., LL.B.
HOWARD UNIVERSITY, WASHINGTON, D.C., U.S.A.

> "Toiling—rejoicing—sorrowing,
>   Onward through life he goes;
> Each morning sees some task begun,
>   Each evening sees its close;
> Something attempted, something done,
>   Has earned a night's repose."
>
> From *The Village Blacksmith.*

CONTENTS

PART I

THE CONFEDERATION OF THE BRITISH WEST INDIES

PART II

THE ANNEXATION OF THE BRITISH WEST INDIAN POSSESSIONS TO THE UNITED STATES OF AMERICA, AND REASONS WHY IT SHOULD NOT BE ENTERTAINED

PART III

FEDERATION WITH COLONIAL
SELF-GOVERNMENT

INTRODUCTION

THE object of this book is to record in a concrete form the aspirations, as gleaned by the writer, of the people of the British West Indian possessions to liberal political freedom; to discourage by just means the growing tendency towards annexation to the United States or Canada; to preach death to taxation without representation and its allied impositions; to request an end to the present antiquated system of government; to suggest reforms in keeping with our advanced civilization so as to destroy the present means whereby a select body of men are enabled successfully to juggle legislation in order that personal ends may be served at the expense and to the detriment of the man behind the " hoe."

In discounting the proposition of annexation it shall be my effort throughout to refrain from condemning the people of the great American Republic as a whole; but it is also my intention not to shield them in principles which are in diametrical opposition to the popular line of thought as applied to alien and negroid races with whom they come in contact in and out of the United States.

Such shortcomings shall be laid bare as plainly and as impartially as my feeble ability will permit, in order that my readers may be reminded of the past, brought face to face with the present, and be forewarned of the future which is upon us.

The engrossing subject of this volume will be the Confederation of the " British West Indian Possessions " with " Colonial Self-Government " as against annexation to the United States of America or Canada.

The topic of annexation of the British West Indies to the United States has undergone most serious contemplation both among Americans in the States and their admirers in these tropical possessions of Great Britain. It therefore behoves those of us who are averse to the move to be on the look-out for the unexpected, in order to be prepared for any emergency ; and also to be in a position successfully to combat all such influence which may have in its endeavour the slightest suspicion of wresting from us the opportunity of obtaining a genuine state of freedom and liberty for one that is a mere shadow.

I shall endeavour to depict as vividly as possible a few of the many difficulties which would follow annexation, including the privations of life, coupled with the total destruction of the spirit of manhood, and of all institutions both civic and politic which are so dear to the heart of civilized man.

The benefits to be derived from Federation with Responsible Government shall be touched upon continually in passing from one subject to another ; thus affording my readers sufficient substantial matter to be enabled to judge beween the two states—Annexation to the United States of America, or Federation with Colonial Self-Government—and to decide in favour of the more profitable.

PART I

THE CONFEDERATION OF THE BRITISH WEST INDIES

CHAPTER I

THE LAW OF THE UNIVERSE

ORDINARILY we use the term "Confederation of the West Indies" to convey the meaning of a union of the British West Indian Possessions, in which are included the rich and undeveloped tracts of land on the mainland of South and Central America, British Guiana, and Honduras.

Among the Latin American Republics the prophecy is that the future of the British West Indian Islands is inseparably bound up with the interests of the United States; that, at the first great crash, British Guiana will be taken over by Venezuela or Brazil, and Mexico will do the honours for British Honduras.

A pretty fine division it would seem to be, and one which is by no means out of place to anticipate; for while these South and Central American countries, awakened out of their long sleep of indolence and revolution, take on the spirit of progression of the twentieth century, and leap forward, they are leaving the British Possessions, on the same continent and in close proximity, hopelessly in the wake, struggling against the tide, bound down by the leaden bonds of a govern-

ment directed from Downing Street many thousands of miles away.

Under such conditions, anything is liable to
happen at any moment, which may be exaggerated
to the point of Englishmen witnessing the sad
spectacle of the flag of a once obsolete Spanish-
American State flying triumphantly over what
was once British territory.

This is an age of rapid developments, and not
a time to sit with folded arms and allow others,
who are not better situated, to leap ahead in the
development of their industries, and in the education of their people to the requirements of the
present civilization. We should not permit ourselves, through lack of concerted action and for
the asking, to be anchored to an antiquated
system of government, which is by no means
adaptable to the present situation.

The nations which were once designated by
backwardness, revolutions, and other internal
strifes, have entered upon a new era, and each
succeeding year adds a page to their history of
modern advancément and achievements.

They have taken on the garb of peace and
prosperity, and have distinctly placed themselves
in the van, while Britain's colonies, on the same
mainland and in neighbouring waters, in spite of
their natural wealth, seem to take on the spirit
of decline and hopelessness.

One has but to take a peep into the great
awakening of Brazil to be convinced that this
tremendous country, rich in mineral resources and

woods, with the fertile valley of the Amazon, capable of producing the world's supply of grain for many centuries, practically unexplored, has stepped forward and demanded a place of recognition in the world's political and commercial affairs.

There are also Chili, Peru, and the Argentine Republic, all of which are making gigantic strides in their internal developments ; and in the near future they will have to be reckoned with in the status of the destiny of nations who are struggling for supremacy as a world power.

The most general and comprehensive definition of " Law " is : " That rule of action prescribed by some superior for the inferior, and which the latter is bound to obey."

This seems to coincide with the interpretation of the law which governs the universe—might is right.

Civilized man still exhibits the traits of the lower animals which are in him. He will subjugate and oppress his fellow men, and even go the length of exterminating those who oppose him in his fight for pre-eminence. The weak must bow to the laws and dictates of the strong ; there is no alternative.

We owe our existence as British subjects to the might of Britain as a great sea-power. How long this band that binds us together and insures our liberty will remain staunch and unbroken depends entirely on the continued position of Great Britain, with regard to her laying down of the " Law."

Should she awake one morning to find that her sea-power has been broken by a crushing onslaught in the night, during an hour of unpreparedness : to find London destroyed by bombs from a hundred Zeppelins ; to find her cities besieged by land and sea ; and the great Channel Fleet, the pride of the nation which has the reputation of the Cossacks before they met the Japanese, broken and battered by the German Navy, and no longer a fighting unit ; we are liable to find ourselves subjects of the Kaiser before another sunset.

In speaking to Captain Johansen, a Norwegian explorer, on the subject of the approaching Anglo-German war, he had this to say : " War is bound to come, and may God help the English. I want to see them win. It would be bad for the world if the Germans are victorious." He is correct, if we are to judge the Germans by their administration in Africa.

The great desire for the Confederation of the British West Indian Possessions is that we want to be a part of the world-wide Empire. We want to be looked upon as part and parcel of the British nation. We want so to equip ourselves as to be in a position to take up our share of the burden of defence of the Empire ; and to preserve the West Indies for the West Indians.*

---

* The term " West Indians " is intended to mean the children of immigrants, both white and black, and their offspring born in the West Indies—the aborigines being almost extinct.

" America for the Americans " has long been the cry of the Yankees. The Canadians have caught the strains of the tune and now they sing " Canada for the Canadians." We hear the same music from Australia, New Zealand, and South Africa. This music is aimed principally at the exclusion of the negro from competing with the white man in these countries. Why, then, should not the West Indian join the grand chorus and sing "The West Indies for the West Indians"? It is an idea which is by no means revolutionary in its purpose when it is considered from an unselfish view-point.

The West Indian, as a negro, is not wanted in the United States of America, which is the home of fifteen million members of his race.

Nowhere in the great British Empire is the negro welcomed unless he has £ s. d. to show as his passport ; and, even when so admitted, his stay could only be tolerated while his money lasts.

Of all the books written on the British West Indies, touching the negro, those written by Englishmen are found to be most venomous and scandalous, with less regard for the truth than writers of other nations. These English writers cull all the evils they can find, and set up a picture which they call a correct type of West Indians' life and custom. One important feature these critics purposely omit, and that is, that every denunciation of the progress of His Majesty's subjects in these parts is a grave reflection on the method of management of these colonies by the British Government.

In British Africa—east, west, north, and south —the original home of the negro, he is eyed by English and Dutch alike. He is refused food and shelter. He is debarred from entering the station of life for which his education fits him. He is denied the right to enjoy the privilege to practise his profession where this brings him in contact with white men.

In the British Navy a man with coloured blood is not wanted, if he aspires to any station above that of an ordinary sailor. The same objection holds good in the Army : thus we who boast ever and always of the might of the English, and glory in our loyalty to the Flag, are left out in the cold on every side, subjugated but not pro- tected. Nevertheless we still sing " Rule, Brit- annia " and " God save the king," while foreigners turn up their nose in polite rebuke at the mere mention of the words, " I am a British subject," as if to say, you ought to be the last creature on earth to talk of it, since it affords you neither protection nor recognition in the broadest sense of the word.

Our only reply to those who thus humble us has been, and shall always be : " We know of none better than Britain, and we love her still and in spite of all."

CHAPTER II

AMERICAN INFLUENCE EXEMPLIFIED

IT is an open secret, if I am permitted to use the phrase, that the American has an inbred antipathy for alien races, and more especially the negro.

It has become a matter of deep concern, a matter to be deplored, that in this modern civilization of the twentieth century, men find it necessary to array themselves on opposite sides on mere matters of difference of colour, creed, and race. Surely our outward show of civilization is but skin deep, which has been bolstered up by an imaginary advancement to a high civilized state, and which fades away as icicles before a melting force when subjected to the most primitive scrutiny.

It is also universally admitted that the American is a poor colonizer, from the fact that he will not readily adapt himself to conditions found outside of his own country, and as a result, his actions in this new sphere have been characterized as the man who—literally speaking—takes the bull by the horns as the simplest and easiest method of overcoming its resistance.

Notwithstanding these existing inequalities, which the Americans themselves by this time realize, it is most noteworthy that that nation is very anxious to adopt or subjugate races which they utterly despise, in their programme of expansion—a circumstance which is by no means compatible with common reason.

We view with no little amount of amazement, the astonishing manner in which they are stealthily injecting their ideas throughout the West Indies and South American Republics, by assuming the rôle of protector, which will in time lead up to permanent occupation.

Even Hayti, the suspicious, which has always been so outspoken against the Yankees, and their aggressive policy towards the West Indies, seems to be doomed to the irresistible advance of this new nation in the arena of land-grabbing tactics.

American financiers are now laying plans for the capture of a part, if not the whole, of Hayti's commerce, which had formerly been left almost entirely in the hands of the Germans; and notwithstanding that a certain section of the native community, spurred on by rivals in the commercial world, has found it necessary to have recourse to vulgar display in this connection, distributing printed handbills with native songs, insinuating vile and ugly things about the invaders, yet they still push on, unmindful of the feeling against them, to the one great end—the final ousting of the Germans from their strong-hold and the intrenching of themselves in the avenues thus made vacant. As soon as these crafty financiers shall have accomplished their primary object in the little Black Republic, as a part of their policy towards the Islands in the Caribbean Sea, then the tragedy of Hawaii will be re-enacted, and we shall, with a wave of the hand, bid good-bye to the sovereignty of Hayti as an independent state.

Toussaint-L'Ouverture recognized this danger while Hayti was yet in her infancy, and probably anticipating the views of the late Herbert Spencer, as the latter dictated them to Baron Kaneko, of Japan, to " keep other races at arm's length as much as possible," it is said that he had inserted in the constitution of the Republic, for whose birth he was mainly responsible, a clause to this effect : No white man, whatever his nationality may be, shall enter into Haytian Ports with the title of proprietor or master, nor shall he be per-mitted to acquire real estate or the rights of a Haytian."

Hayti has, up to the present stage profited by this far-seeing lesson, set out for the benefit of coming generations by the father of their country ; and the day that they depart from its precepts, by allowing the Americans to gain a foothold in their country, this memorable clause, written with the blood of their forefathers, which history says flowed from their bodies in such quantities that the sea around the land was red with it, will necessarily have to undergo great modification if not complete abrogation.

It appears, therefore, that in addition to what has been already said, the colonies of Great Britain, France, and Holland will sooner or later be dominated by this young giant of the west— the United States of America.

How long will these European possessions, which geologically belong to the American continent, remain free of that fearful contaminating influence is the great question which all those who are interested in their destiny are clamouring to solve.

I venture to predict that the crisis cannot be delayed very much longer, judging from the many surrounding circumstances which tend to give colour to the popular belief that American mastery of the West Indies is *jure divino*. The eagle has unsheathed his talons and is ready for the fray. Will there be a fray at all ? Is the game worth the candle ?

What will England say when she is asked to part from her West Indian Colonies for love, policy, or money ? It must be remembered that within the past century these possessions have been rather a burden to her than a treasure ; that she has practically lost all interest in them ; and that their only value to the British crown, up to the time of the discovery of oil in the land of the " Humming Bird," was to serve as a feeding ground for high-salaried officials.

There are those who say that Britain will dispose of her West Indian possessions for what they are worth, rather than have them serve as a bone of contention with her natural ally. Others contend that she will not give them up for love nor for money, but will hang on for old acquaintance sake, if for no other purpose. Which will win ? Personally, I am inclined to share with those of the former opinion, for it would be a circumstance as much to be deplored as our annexation to that great Republic, to see these two great English-speaking nations at loggerheads over a few patches of thirsty clay.

This impending state of affairs can, however, be very nicely avoided ; and its solution lies seemingly in the confederation of these British possessions in the West Indies under colonial self-government.

Had not this been foreseen and provided against by Canada, we might have been pained to read of her as what was " once a British Colony forming a part of the United States of America "; but, instead of that, we find her to-day, by taking timely action, a great British self-governing colony, more English than she ever was, and showing every indication that she will always remain so.

There has been considerable talk in some sections about annexation of the West Indies to Canada, but even if the very unlikely happened, and the Dominion found herself in a position to adopt us as her ward, she would be deterred in her purpose, out of fear of displeasing the United

States. There is no longer any question of a doubt that the United States is a power to be reckoned with in shaping the destiny of the West Indies.

The people of the American continent look with displeasure at a foreign power holding territory in the waters of their domain ; and were it not for the diplomacy and strength of Great Britain as a maritime power, she might long have ceased to own possessions in the Western Hemisphere.

This feeling among the Americans, that to them should belong everything on this side of the Atlantic, is as natural as the feeling among the Japanese that everything in the far East should be commanded by Japan.

The changes that war may bring are many and calamitous, and but while Britain remains unconquered or unfettered by a crushing war, so long shall we remain subjects of the King, at his pleasure ; but if a conflict comes, and the unexpected happens, no one knows whether we shall, when the battle-clouds have passed, find ourselves subjugated by Yankees or Germans.

That this dark war-cloud has been gathering for some time, and which may have reached such a stage of maturity as to make the invasion of the British Isles, on paper, a matter of fact, leaves little room for doubt in the minds of the most astute of her statesmen, who are familiar with the methods of the would-be invaders. This is no new story. It has been the prophecy of years by the world's greatest rulers and generals, comprising such men as Napoleon, Crispi, Bismarck, Beaconsfield, and many others of modern times.

Soon Britain will have to fight for her very existence ; and it might become imperative for her to strike swiftly the first crushing blow, with all her strength, in the interest of the preservation of her commercial and maritime supremacy, or be relegated to the place of a second-class power.

Every British subject, no matter if he is residing in the most remote part of the Empire, wants to be counted upon as contributing to its impelling force whenever it is found necessary to strike that " blow."

There should be no conscription : when war comes, we want, every one of us, to feel that we are a material part of the world-wide Empire ; that we have something to protect. We would like to lay down our lives, not because we are forced to do so, but because we feel that the cause is a common one.

It would indeed be a sad plight if British Colonial policy, as it is administered in her Crown Colonies, should damp our loyalty to such an extent as to prevent us coming voluntarily, *en masse*, on every necessary occasion to offer our services in the defence of the Empire.

We want to live as animate beings—living representatives of British might ; and to die, if needs be, as soldiers of the King in the defence of any cause that may call forth our assistance.

This feeling, however, can never be seriously entertained by a subjugated people who are even denied a voice in the government of the affairs of their native land. Such a people are nothing less than slaves ; and until they are free men, it would be folly for them to feel that they seriously constitute a material part of the British Empire.

The pronoun " we " is frequently, possibly too frequently, used in our remarks as West Indians on the great British Empire. It is a mistake, a perversion of the English language, by those who do not realize their proper status. Only Englishmen, and those of the great self-governing Colonies are justified conscientiously in using the collective.

CHAPTER III

OUR TERMS OF CONFEDERATION

IF we accept the suggestion that federation is the only visible means of checking the drifting tendency of the West Indies towards annexation to the United States, and its associate evils, which under present conditions seems inevitable ; then it would be quite unnecessary to produce any further argument in substantiation ; but as there are many who are in favour of annexation, and others who hail for Confederation, in order to treat the subject impartially, it becomes necessary to show reasons for and against.

It shall be my endeavour to point out to my readers in as convincing a manner as lies in my power, the benefits that are likely to follow federation, and the evils attendant on annexation of these West Indian possessions of Great Britain to the United States of America.

The scheme of confederation is not a new one to the British West Indies. It was proposed to the Lesser Antilles but a short time ago, and those that accepted the conditions as put forward by the commissioners seem to have been materially benefited.

The Island of Tobago choosing between two evils—that of facing total bankruptcy or forming a union with a sister colony—was one of the lot which entered into the new combination with desirable results.

She accepted the suggestion to be linked to Trinidad, and experience has shown that she has been greatly benefited by the amalgamation.

The additional or new phase in the re-presentation of this question is to be found in the addition of the proposition of Colonial self-government in connection therewith ; and a more general and extensive Federation embracing all the British Colonies in these parts. Nor is this the first appeal that has been made from the West Indies in the interest of self-government.

In the year 1887 the Home Government was petitioned in the interest of this great, civilized, and just cause by the inhabitants of Trinidad, British West Indies, and although the demand was made for a very mild form, yet it fully demonstrated that the people were quite alive to the impositions heaped upon them by the continued policy of taxation without representation —a " state " which has been completely outgrown in the West Indies many generations ago.

It can be positively stated, in one breath, that the British West Indian desires no federation, if it cannot be proposed on a liberal basis.

A confederation which would mean simply a centralization of the revenues, combined with the present form of Colonial Administration, is neither sought nor desired ; and any proposal on such lines would, I believe, be rejected by the people to a man.

On the other hand, if the proposition comes with self-government, it would find but few opponents ; and these would be confined to the present office-holders, and others who desire to see the colonies pass under American rule. Fortunately, these two factions do not comprise the hundredth part of the population.

It is not my expectation that this book should be treated as a guide on matters appertaining to confederation of the British West Indian possessions, or that whatever ideas are laid down herein are infallible : it simply expresses the view of one person on the subject.

Nor do I expect every one to concur with me, for to anticipate this would be to make one of the fourteen mistakes of life—" To expect uniformity of actions, or to attempt to set up one's own standard of right or wrong, and to expect every one to conform to it."

I sincerely desire to avoid that error throughout this work, and if it appears at any time to my readers that I have attempted to assert myself by laying down a rule as being infallible, such a mistake has been absolutely unavoidable.

In giving my version of the benefits which, in my opinion, would be derived from a union of the British Colonies in the West Indies, I am by no means endeavouring to force every one into line with my convictions. What I most desire to effect is harmony in thoughts along similar lines, preparatory to the relentless campaign which is to follow, in our efforts to accomplish the desired end.

One of the greatest drawbacks to the advancement of the West Indians in general, is their strict adherence to parochialism, a condition in which one thinks only of himself, and the things in his immediate surroundings, without a thought for one instant that there are other places and people to whom he or she could be of some benefit, simply by an exercise of freedom of thought and action.

As a result the observer finds, to his astonishment and regret, that the people residing in one borough are absolutely ignorant of what is going on across the line. We also find this state of perfect indifference among the people inhabiting the various islands and possessions.

The Jamaican and Demerarian are for the most part ignorant of what is going on in Barbados, St. Vincent, or Trinidad, etc., and vice versa. The people of one island know little or nothing, and care less about the product, customs, resources, religion, or law of a sister colony, and they view the migration of the inhabitants of one possession to another as a foreign element, and proceed to set up barriers for their exclusion.

This condition of stagnation of the mind is most deplorable, and should not be encouraged, if we are to move abreast with the times and to prepare ourselves for that change which is so very necessary to our future existence.

" Our terms of confederation " can have no better definition than " a government by the people for the people."

CHAPTER IV

THE PROGRESSIVE AGE

THE time when we must do the thinking for ourselves is at hand.

Heretofore we have had (either of our own accord, or by training) to rely on others—the Home Government—to fill for us this very important office, which is the heritage of every civilized individual.

This being unmistakably an age of progression, we find that it does not take quite a century to achieve one's aim.

Things that have occupied a number of men for many years are now being accomplished in infinitely less time, and why? Because the example has been set. It remains, therefore, for us to copy the things that are best adapted to our present needs, and to disregard those containing elements which tend to retard our progress.

In this way we gain a decided advantage over the pioneers of modern civilization. The following is a striking example :—In the year 1854, a little over fifty years ago, the United States, in the person of Commodore Perry, backed up by a few war-ships, knocked at the door of distant Japan in the name of humanity and the " open-door policy." Forty years after, we find this little Eastern nation achieving the hitherto impossible task of humbling the hordes of China ; but the Occidental world found an excuse for this wonderful achievement, by attributing the defeat of China to her internal corruption and dislike for modern civilization and custom. Ten years after her war with China, when every one thought that she was still suffering from the effects of the campaign, she threw the world into a fit of nervous convulsion by engaging in a death struggle with the mightiest nation in all Europe—the nation which defied the French and English in the Crimea—and again she was victorious.

This time the nations were willing to concede a place to her in the ranks of first-class powers, because she had successfully completed a task which they (the nations), combined, would have willingly shirked, had it fallen to their lot to accomplish.

It was then fully and practically demonstrated that those who copy the customs and acts of the highest civilized states, although piratical in principle, have many things from which to choose, besides the absolute superiority of position in being able to leave strictly alone those elements which are considered immaterial to their progress. This is precisely what the Japanese have done and are still doing. All this took place in less than two generations, admitting that the space

of thirty years is acknowledged as constituting
that period.

To those who look forward to a general Federation of the British possessions in the Western
Hemisphere under colonial self-government as
an evil day, I desire to say that these colonies,
which have had the tutelage of the most dis-
ciplinary form of government for over two centuries, are in just as good a position as Japan, if
not a better, when she began the adoption of
progressive ideas, inasmuch as we do not cherish
the ambition to become a world power.

Sixty years ago the population of Australia
numbered only 400,000, but by careful attention
to sanitation, and by enacting measures conducive
to a desirable class of immigrants, we find her
to-day with nearly 5,000,000 souls, and an over-
sea trade totalling up to £114,000,000 sterling
annually.

It was in the year 1852 that the scheme of
federation of the Australian Colonies first dawned
upon the people, but it was not before 1886 that
the agitation assumed an acute stage throughout
the length and breadth of the land.

In the same year the Imperial Parliament gave
its permission for the Federal Council to convene
at Hobart to deliberate on the question. Three
years later (1889) Sir Henry Parkes, the then
Premier of New South Wales, called a National
Convention to discuss the scheme.

In 1891, two years later, the Federal Council
of Australia met at Sydney, at which meeting

all the colonies were represented, and a Federal Constitution was drawn up.

This was not the end, however, for, after four years of complete inactivity, another conference was held at Hobart, when it was unanimously voted that the Federation of Australia was the most pertinent question in the politics of the country.

Notwithstanding these various attempts, satisfactory progress was not made until the year 1896, and finally, on January 1st, 1901, the Federation of the Colonies became a *fait accompli*.

In these days, however, when everything seems to be characterized by its rapidity of progression, it is to be hoped that when the subject of the Union of the West Indies (British) makes its initial bow to the British public in its appeal for responsible government, it will become a reality in less than five years.

The signs of the time are fully exemplified in the rise of the Dominion of Canada from a dependency to a self-governing colony, and, last but not least, a naval power in two years.

Every West Indian who has been keeping in touch with the latest Imperial developments, feels that the time is fast approaching when we shall be asked by the mother country to take to ourselves the responsibilities of care-taking, as having attained our majority.

Whether we should sit patiently and await the pleasure of the Home Government, or whether we should, by anticipating the event, move forward to meet it, will be one of the subjects of discussion in this book.

Great Britain has long realized that, unless she rids herself of the immediate burden of her colonies and converts them into allies that will feel and share their adequate part of the Empire's burden, she would in a short time be called upon to deal with some of the problems which confronted Spain in the management of her numerous dependencies, when she practically ruled the greater part of the earth's surface ; and which reduced her to almost nothingness.

Nations, like stars, have their seasons of eclipse, from which but few emerge to accomplish their final destiny. Like individuals, they are actors upon a stage. They appear, play their part well or badly, hear the applause or hooting of the audience, only to pass off and give place to others.

Rome, the greatest of them all, is no longer the terror of nations. Her power is now such a thing of the past, that the Romans of to-day were vanquished by the Abyssinians—a supposed backward African race.

Next came Spain, who possibly actually ruled more of the earth's surface than did Rome; but she too is only a memory to-day of her former self.

France under Napoleon tried in Roman fashion to gather all the countries of the world under the banner of the Tricolour, which brought her to grief.

Britain, of all the conquering nations, has been able to keep her acquired territory intact. She has been the grandest actress of them all, but her day is near at hand. This she realizes and is preparing to meet it—a foresight which had never occurred to the Romans or the Spaniards. It is by the adoption of this timely measure that she will be saved from the extinction which has overwhelmed her predecessors as world-powers.

The wars that marked the ruin of former world-rulers will one day overtake Britain. Indeed, it (the ruin) seems near at hand. Will she be able to defend her shores, and at the same time grant ample protection to her dissected possessions scattered all over the world, unless there is a re-organization ?

When England creates for her West Indian possessions the position of self-governing colonies, the people who inhabit these possessions will no longer feel themselves mere subjects of the King, but Englishmen who are living in dissected parts of the Empire.

The nation which takes an alien people and educates them up to a certain standard, directly or indirectly, creates a new state for such a people, and consequently cannot expect them, after more than three-quarters of a century of freedom, to be the same blind, unthinking, and subservient beings as when the light of knowledge first dawned upon them. Such a condition would undoubtedly be a great reflection upon the teacher.

The West Indians have reached a stage, where they now halt and demand some consideration which can neither be put off nor neglected for any great length of time.   I feel that if the Home Government does not take the initiative, it will sooner or later be asked by the West Indians themselves to settle the question, or face the issue of annexation to a foreign power.

It cannot be denied that there is a strong undercurrent feeling of dissatisfaction with the present method of administration throughout the British West Indies.

They have not shown their dissatisfaction and disapproval in " Boer Style " simply because they have been differently trained ; but how long it shall be possible to hold them in the leash, without a change in the policy as it is dictated from Downing Street is a question which the future alone can answer.   It suffices to say that the situation, if unchanged, will not long be unattended with grave possibilities.

If the colonies succeed in getting what they want, it will be a signal for an era of great awakening for them :   on the other hand, should they fail in their first appeal, it would not mean death to the cause, but a renewal of the attack with increased vigour.

Why should the thought of failure be allowed to complicate this just cause, which is full of advantage to both parties concerned ?

Have we not been as loyal as the Australians, Canadians, or Africanders ?   Did we not come forward as loyal subjects and offer our services as volunteers when all Europe, united with the Boers, now a loyal and self-governing people, threatened to crush Britain's power in Africa ?

Can a people show their devotion to their sovereign more than by offering up their lives for the glory of the Empire ?

Is it not with negro soldiers, chiefly from these colonies, that England has won victories and territories from the Cape to Cairo ?

Have the millions of negroes and creoles in these possessions ever given the mother country cause for anxiety ? True enough, there have been petty strifes, but at no time was the sovereignty of Britain threatened in the slightest degree.

Why, then, should we not be treated with the same consideration, at least, as the Boers, whose declaration and pursuit of war against England's suzerainty rocked the Empire from stem to stern, and caused the mother country the loss of many of her best sons, and millions in money ?

Britain has profited by Spain's blunders and poor diplomacy in the government of her colonies ; and she has wisely embarked upon a scheme of regenerating herself by granting self-government to them, in which programme she will not be misled to make any exception.

With the United West Indies placed on a sound footing, and anchored under the parental protection and guidance of the mother country, an epoch of renewed vigour would be witnessed among her colonies in the Atlantic and Caribbean Sea.

" England ! the time is come when thou shouldst wean
  Thy heart from its emasculating focd ;
  The truth should now be better understood ;
  Old things have been unsettled ; we have seen
  Fair seed-time, better harvest might have been
  But for thy trespasses ; and at this day,
  If for Greece, Egypt, India, Africa
  Aught good were destined, thou wouldst step between.
  England ! all nations in this charge agree :
  But worse, more ignorant in love than hate,
  Far, far more abject is thine enemy :
  Therefore the wise pray for thee, though the freight
  Of thy offences be a heavy weight :
  Oh, grief ! that earth's best hopes rest all with thee ! "

                                        WORDSWORTH.

CHAPTER V

RELATION OF SELF-GOVERNING COLONIES TO THE MOTHER COUNTRY

BEFORE entering upon the subject of " Relation of Self-Governing Colonies to the Mother Country," it would be most refreshing to review the moral and spiritual advancement of the British Empire during the present century.

To begin with, education has made immeasurable strides ; prison reforms have been perfected ; law and justice have been more firmly established upon their respective thrones ; religion has been greatly imbued with light, charity, and love ; and there has been on every hand, through the efforts of our late sovereigns—Queen Victoria the Good, and King Edward the Peacemaker—such a forward movement towards the realization of universal brotherhood as the previous century had scarcely dreamed of or hoped to see.

With the declaration that turbulent India is to be given a constitution, as a preliminary to being launched out as another great self-governing colony, carrying with it another example of the unquestionable fairness of British Colonial policy, the wisdom of the politicians is again demonstrated.

At this juncture one is constrained to feel that the limit has been fairly reached, and while we silently appreciate the carrying out of this most worthy act towards India, it is plain that the Home Government has unjustly superseded, in the granting of this form of relief, some of her most deserving colonies. I refer to her West Indian possessions.

To those who profess to know something about the pretensions of the Indian people, the question naturally suggests itself : Will India, after obtaining the highest gift that is possible for a mother country to grant to a daughter colony (self-government), be satisfied with her new position, or will she one day strike out for absolute freedom and decide to shake off British control altogether ? Not possible ! No ! ! Not if she is far-seeing.

The balance of power would be so thoroughly out of her favour should she decide to take a plunge in the dark, that regrets, remorse, and confusion would reign in the place where liberty and happiness should have absolute sway. India would find herself beset by the same perplexities, as an independent nation, as those which would most certainly confront Canada as a sovereign power.

The Dominion as an independent nation would exist only at the will of the teeming millions of the United States who, breaking their bounds, would overrun her in less than ten years, and thus so completely submerge her individuality as to return her to a position similar to that of a Crown Colony, if not a stage below.

This would be the exact position in which India would find herself, if, after receiving her constitutional powers, she eventually strikes out for independence, and is successful in the attempt ; for with Japan on one hand seeking for expansion, and Russia on the other, eager to obtain an outlet to the sea, her position would be short-lived.

The only salvation, therefore, of the British self-governing colonies lies in their keeping under the ever-protecting wing of the mother country, and by exerting every possible means in their power to strengthen and preserve Britain's supremacy on the seas for their own safety.

As British self-governing colonies, which form a sort of daughterhood, their external relations and internal development, guided, helped, and protected by the strong arm of the mother country, would be secure to an unparalleled degree ; but let them divert from this, and attempt to assert themselves, and foreign domination stares them in the face.

There is also another side of the question, and that is, What would be the position of the other self-governing colonies should one of their number, determining to terminate her relationship with the mother country, declare for absolute independence ?

The action which would be taken by Great

Britain and the loyal colonies in such an emergency can readily be surmised by those who are familiar with the history of the American Civil War, and our recent South African Campaign.

Many persons of undoubted intelligence have gone off their heads, being misled by the popular idea that the American Civil War was brought about for the emancipation of the negroes.

This is not so. It is true that the question of the expansion of the slave trade was incident to the great struggle between the north and south ; but the real cause was the attempt of the Southern States to secede from the union when their programme for the further advancement of this slave traffic in states where the custom had either died out or was not known was rejected. This war was the result of an effort to keep the Union intact ; and would, without doubt and in all probability, be the course that would be adopted in the event of an attempt being made by one of the self-governing colonies to break away from the bonds of the Empire.

The recent speech of Lord Charles Beresford at a banquet in Canada to the effect that, " If the Dominion decides to withdraw from the Empire, no one would seek to prevent her," is totally unfounded and without an analogy in the history of nations.

There is scarcely any difference between the privileges of a self-governing colony under the British system, and that of the exercise of the functions of an independent nation, except that in the latter case the question of defence against invasion must be combated single-handed ; a responsibility which carries with it a great national burden, while in the former it would fall upon some one else, and the colony would still reap all the benefits of a sovereign state.

It is the general opinion that Britain has greatly prolonged her life as the world's greatest power for many more centuries by her acts of leniency in extending responsible government to most of her colonies ; and she has thus removed every symptom of discontent from the breasts of her subjects who are beneficiaries of this new and benevolent policy.

To illustrate more properly the relation of the self-governing colonies to the mother country, it is necessary to elucidate their positive inability to take care of themselves against nations stronger in military and naval equipments, and to this end I cite the case of the " Canada-Alaska boundary dispute." At the time of the controversy, Canada being of the belief that her contention was right, and that she, by a process known only to herself, was sufficiently powerful to grapple with her giant neighbour the United States, was eager to provoke a war.

If we judge the situation by the most elementary process of comparing the strength of two separate bodies, it is evident that Canada could not win in such a fight.

Whether she counted upon embroiling the mother country as a natural sequence, or risking what she thought it her right to risk (Canadian territory) and moving on her own account, leaving England to act in whatever way she thought fit, has never been satisfactorily forecast.

Britain, however, seeing the danger ahead, soon took a hand in the controversy, and, setting her foot on this very ambitious scheme of that dependency, she quickly brought her to her senses.

This move on the part of England produced a flurry among a large number of Canadians, and there were talks of giving away Canadian territory ; and of Great Britain bending her knees to the United States. These talks were only silenced when the Dominion was informed by the mother country that the question of the Canada-Alaska boundary was a matter which concerned the Imperial Government alone, and which must take precedence over colonial matters. Realizing its true status, the Dominion Government reluctantly yielded its point : thus England's diplomacy and far-sightedness again asserted itself, and what would have otherwise been a calamitous war between these two great North-American countries with far-reaching consequences, was avoided ; Canada being without army or navy at the time.

Had she been a sovereign power, a conflict would have been inevitable, the fruits of which would be the turning backwards of the clock of progress, for at least half a century, as far as the Dominion is concerned ; and to-day the Stars and Stripes would be seen floating gaily over acquired Canadian territory, if not above the citadel of Quebec.

On the other hand, occupying her present position, as a British self-governing colony, had war been forced upon her by the United States, that country would have had to reckon with the might of Great Britain, and Greater Britain beyond the seas.

The safety, therefore, of the self-governing colonies lies in clinging to British protection as long as she is able to maintain her supremacy on the ocean ; and it is to their advantage to see that her position as the world's ruling power is unassailed.

The greatest minds among the public men in Canadian affairs have presumably realized this benefit, if we are to judge by what *The Telegraph* of St. John's, N.B., has to say on the subject.

Says this paper :

" It is not our connection with the Empire that renders necessary the expenditure we contemplate. If we were out of the Empire we should have to spend much more on our Army and Navy than we shall do now, or else Canada would have to abandon her national existence and become a spineless ward of the United States, or an actual part of the Republic.

" With the adoption of the new naval policy, we shall not, as some prophets suppose, drift away from the Empire, but shall become more and more closely identified with it in purpose and sentiment, without, in any sense, forgoing or diminishing our self-governing powers.

" Knowing that insurance is necessary, we are merely undertaking to pay our share.

" We do not expect a fire, but we shall not on that account allow the policy to lapse."

The *Toronto Globe* has this to say about the Dominion's Naval Policy which is condemned as unwholesome by the press of the United States :

" Perhaps after a time both countries (speaking of the relative position of England and Germany in their naval armament contest) may come to a better understanding and the present ruinous competition be brought to a termination.

" Until the competition ceases the world may be assured that the mother country will not slacken her determination to retain her unquestioned supremacy, and in this she will be more strongly supported by the daughter nations with every added year."

These are Canada's answers to America's efforts to discourage a Canadian naval policy, and a warning to Germany that it must be " the whole hog or none."

Could such loyalty have come from a people if they were subjugated by the Crown Colony system of government which is nothing less than autocratic in principle, and a gigantic farce perpetrated upon a law-abiding, intelligent, and peace-loving people ?   Never ! Never ! !

No white race would stand for taxation without representation, and this has been demonstrated over and over again.

They very promptly resort to shots and shells, not stones and sticks, as a means of settling their differences, and for that very tendency they merit the respect of the world wherever they abide ; while the negro race in a similar situation is discounted and oppressed, through the want of sufficient courage to face the ordeal of freedom or extermination.

We do not seek the " freedom " that would destroy the link that binds us to the mother country, but we solicit the liberty of self-government, whereby we may be possessed with the means of checking the present unjustifiable policy towards the West Indies as they are dictated from Downing Street.

PART II

THE ANNEXATION OF THE BRITISH WEST INDIAN POSSESSIONS TO THE UNITED STATES OF AMERICA, AND REASONS WHY IT SHOULD NOT BE ENTERTAINED

CHAPTER VI

THE ANNEXATION, AND REASONS WHY IT
SHOULD NOT BE ENTERTAINED

THERE are so many objections to advance against
the annexation of the British West Indian possessions to the United States that the commercial
benefits which would be derived from such a union
are completely overshadowed.

One of the main points at issue is the standard
of inequality (set up by the Americans with respect to other persons) based on colour, creed,
and race, irrespective of qualifications.

With the Americans you must be White!
White!! White!!! You must be white to be
truthful and honest. You must be white to hold
any position of trust outside of the political
realm; and more than all, the American white
man is rated, in the United States, at a higher
premium than any other member of the Caucasian
race, and so it is wherever the Stars and Stripes
float as the controlling power.

In this connection, with reference to race hatred,
it is not the negro alone that is singled out for
attack. The Jews, the Chinese, and the Japanese
come in for their proportionate share of ostracism,

43

with the exception that it is administered to these in a much milder form.

About the two last-named races we shall not concern ourselves at this time. It suffices to say that even though they find it an up-hill work to get along in social circles, in localities where a certain element of Yankee * influence is predominant, they are infinitely much better treated than members of the negro race.

The Chinese, Japanese, East Indian, and other yellow races, all take precedence over the negro in all questions of just and equitable treatment under the Stars and Stripes, except in cases of citizenship.

It might, however, be interesting to my readers to say a word or two on the Jewish problem in the United States, before passing on to the main subject, as members of this *illustrious race* are well looked upon, even in the best English society, and comprise the influential section of our West Indian merchant community.

In justice to the Jews it must be said that the opposition against them is maintained only in the most exclusive circles ; there they are confronted by the greatest obstacles imaginable in their attempt to make any headway, and this, in spite of wealth.

Much of this feeling against them is engendered through their creed and the stringent exercise of

* The term " Yankee " is used herein to cover Americans in a general way. Strictly speaking the word is confined only to the Northerners.

thrift for which the race is characteristic. And notwithstanding that Jewish wealth is an important factor in the economic and political affairs of the country, they find themselves hopelessly segregated in matters of broad social equality.

As an illustration : There are many hotels, club houses, and summer resorts in and around the cosmopolitan city of New York, which will not entertain members of the Hebrew race, and it can be stated without the slightest fear of contradiction that hotels and boarding-houses which are frequented by Jewish families are never patronized by the better and middle-class native American.

The candidature of a Jew for any political position is never taken seriously, except in some section of the Southern States, where they practically own everything dead and living within the horizon. A most striking example of the consideration which is given to Jewish candidates for public offices in the United States is seen in the many strenuous efforts of a prominent New York journalist, millionaire, and owner of several other newspapers all over the country, to capture any political office, ranging from mayor of his native State to the Presidency of the Republic.

There is no room for doubt that this millionaire newspaper owner is an honest and well-thinking man ; one who is earnest in his endeavours ; and a man with the people's cause at heart. But by reason of his nationality, all his efforts, even though backed by unlimited capital, have ended in ignominious failures.

The climax of discrimination against Jews was reached when a Hebrew multi-millionaire, who owns more property in the city of New York than any other resident, was turned out of a city restaurant without a meal, simply because no Jews were allowed its accommodations, and the proprietor could not see his way clear to make an exception.

The result was that this man of vast wealth left the United States never to return ; and went to England and became a naturalized subject of Great Britain.

CHAPTER VII

ANNEXATION AND THE NEGRO

HAVING regard for the future of the negroes who have been brought up under British rule, no one could for a moment contemplate the annexation of the British West Indian possessions to the United States of America, without some thought for the large negro population which comprises the bulk of the inhabitants of these islands, knowing the bitter racial feelings which the Yankees cherish and cultivate against the coloured race.

As every one knows, over nine-tenths of the people of the West Indies are of negro descent, and, consequently, of mixed blood. Their freedom of action and liberty have gone on unrestricted for generations. Some of these people have long forgotten that negro blood is discernible by the naked eye in their veins. They have taken up the guise and demeanour of the Europeans, with the title of " white " to boot. And imitating the " jackdaw in peacock's feathers," they " strut along " among the illiterate under the garb of " white men."

To such the Americans apply the distinctive name of " West Indian Whites," which is interpreted to mean persons who are posing as what in reality they are not.

These " West Indian Whites," were they to be told that they are negroes, with a view of circumscribing their sphere of action or social standing, would be so rudely shocked at the seemingly uncalled for remark, that they would actually have to stop and look at their hands before they would realize what was really meant.

If the annexation were to be brought about, would it be a benefit or a curse to our West Indian population ? Those who are opposed to Yankee mastery hold to the latter. They prefer to content themselves with the " ills " with which they are familiar rather than rush to new and untried ones.

The annexationists maintain that American occupation would be a blessing to these possessions. They hold that the presence of the Yankees as controlling factors would exercise an influence for good upon the black, yellow, mulatto, and quadroon, and bring them together for united action, thus proving a blessing in disguise. Which is right ? The position being somewhat problematical, I am, as a third party, forced to take up the attitude of the " man on the fence," leaving the question to be decided by my readers.

The class to which I desire to draw special attention, is that which has already been alluded to under the designation of " West Indian Whites," and their connection with the effect which annexation would have upon this class with that *one drop* of negro blood coursing through their veins.

In the West Indies this grade of coloured people has been allowed to go on, practically unquestioned, for more than a century, with regard to which class they do really belong.

This has been so because no one cares, and it wouldn't matter anyway, whether a certain Mr. or Mrs. So-and-so, who maintains that *he or she is lily-white*, but whose mother or grandmother is known to everyone as a brown or mulatto woman, possesses *one* or a *million* drops of negro blood.

In these His Majesty's possessions, what is most urgently necessary is the qualification which fits one for the society one seeks to enter. The chief feature in this qualification is money. Colour does not seem to be a very serious menace, and a good many shortcomings are thereby overlooked. But would this state of affairs be tolerated under annexation ?

I emphatically say *no !* Things would be compelled to undergo material change through force of circumstances, resulting in the relegation into the negro ranks of a people, who now feel themselves secure from social ostracism.

Already an American novelist of note, who has made several sojourns in the West Indies, has seen fit to point out in the public press, what she calls a " weakness among West Indian negroes, who think themselves white, in their endeavour to be always pushing their noses in the face of

white women, as if they were really white men."
For whom is this meant ? Surely not the black
man, for he certainly has no such pretensions.

This condemnation coming from one, a lady,
who has been fêted by " our whites," who had
up to the time of the publication of her statement
felt that they had succeeded in carrying away
her feminine heart and passed into the " White
Circle " unrecognized, under cover of the effect
upon the skin of the much maligned tropical sun,
must necessarily make them sit up and think.
Isn't this proof enough that they have been discovered at their old game ?

It is this class of West Indian aristocracy that
would be the greatest sufferers. They would be
singled out for attack on every occasion, as experience has taught those who have had an
opportunity of studying the racial and social
problems connected with Yankee civilization.

There are many persons who are at present
merely tolerated by the Americans, who visit the
West Indies as a winter resort, out of delicacy
for the situation, being temporary sojourners in
another man's country.

Many natives are consequently misled, by the
calm exterior of these visitors, to conclude (those
of us who are posing as white people) that they
have escaped the scrutiny of the practised eyes of
these negro-haters with whom they come in contact ; but all such persons are bound on a mis-
taken errand.

The American people, as a whole, are very

keen on the matter of colour diagnosis, particularly so among those who have lived in the south and south-west.

While Mr. —— was chief of the Materials and Supplies Department of the Isthmian Canal Commission, with offices at Mount Hope, Canal Zone, he had occasion to call on the author of this book, who was at the time engaged in the practice of medicine in the Canal Zone, etc., relative to a young woman who sought employment in his household. The young lady, a Jamaican, had always been known as a white person, and appeared for ordinary purposes as white as the chief himself : but no sooner had I produced her photograph which had come into my possession as a part of the application, than he pronounced her a coloured woman, and on that account refused to employ her in his household. I subsequently made personal inquiries and found out to my satisfaction that the chief was minutely correct. It was only *one drop* of coloured blood, but that was enough to cause a shudder to run through the frame of this man of prejudice, who declared that his cook and his butler, who were Irish, would rebel as soon as it was discovered that the " Jamaican-white " had coloured blood in her veins, and that this would greatly inconvenience his family. The position for which the young lady applied was that of a humble waiting-maid.

The pure-blooded negro and those who are sufficiently dark of skin as to bear no doubt as to the identity of the race to which he or she belongs are, in a measure, in a safe position; but there is great danger, unmistakably so, awaiting those who are possessed of the diabolical " one drop of negro blood " when brought in direct contact with the Americans.

Although the person with his or her *one drop* may not be cognizant of it, the average American is capable of detecting it and will go far out of his way to have such an individual removed from the exclusive " White Circle " by having him or her segregated and relegated back to the ranks of the blackest negro, in every walk of life in which the white race participates.

One has not to go far to find substantiation of this charge, nor is the custom so ancient that the present generation can hope for some leniency from the American people. Indeed, not longer ago than May 28, 1910, an incident which occurred during that very month in Washington, district of Columbia, the *nation's capital*, was recorded in the New Orleans *Daily Picayune*, and reproduced by the Colon *Starlet* dated June 7, 1910. Under the head of " Colour Line Problem " it says :

" The question how much negro blood is necessary to classify a person as coloured under the School Law of the District of Columbia may soon be submitted to the courts for determination, says the New Orleans *Daily Picayune*.

" Early on the morning of the 28th ult. the Board of Education, after wrangling for hours over the proposition to admit Isabel Wall, a child of seven, to the Public Schools, decided that not-withstanding her appearance was white, without a sign of negro blood, there was some evidence to the effect that in the child's ancestors, a mulatto great-grandmother appeared, and therefore she must be classed as coloured."

This infant was consequently expelled and hurled back to the negro ranks, to share the same fate, because of that *one drop of negro blood.*

Those who are at present crying out for annexation of the British West Indian possessions, in part or whole, to the United States, must be credited with total ignorance of the real situation.

In religious matters also, it would appear, judging from the rigid exclusiveness carried out by the Americans on the basis of colour, that the God of the white man is not the God of the negro ; and while they (the whites) cannot be charged with actually promulgating such a doctrine, yet their actions speak louder than words.

In the United States there are the white church and the negro church, by which is meant churches for white persons only, and churches for negroes only, ranging through the various shades from the black to the " white negro."

No distinction whatsoever is made on account of wealth, position, or previous standing. The rule is applied without exception.

In all schools, trains, street-cars, parks, and other public and private institutions, including theatres, south of the Mason and Dixon line, the strict segregation of the *negroes* from the whites is enforced by statutes.

If by mistake a negro came to the door of a " white church " on a Sunday morning, his reception would depend altogether on the temper of the beadle.

If this unfortunate occurrence happens at a time when the newspapers all over the country are crying out for the death of the " Negro Brute," the caller would be summarily dealt with by the man at the door, without expecting any redress from the courts ; but if, on the other hand, temporary outward tranquillity exists between the races, the individual might be dismissed, with the information to go to the " White House."

To those who do not understand the extent of the hatred and contempt which the American people hold for the negro, the insinuation that one may find a negro church in the White House (Presidential Palace) would seem a huge joke ; but behind this apparently harmless assertion a bomb is hurled at the entire negro race with great bitterness.

This " White House " phrase has its origin in a little political episode which occurred at the executive mansion some years ago during the incumbency of Theodore Roosevelt, a president of the United States, when he invited Booker T. Washington, the great negro-educator and leader, to lunch with him.

The mere fact that the Chief Executive condescended to sit at table with a coloured man created such a stir in the nation, that it was at one time seriously thought that this *little affair* would cause the assassination of Mr. Roosevelt. Yet Roosevelt is no lover of the negro.

In Congress the incident was taken up with vigour, and debated as an item of national importance. In the Senate the President's action was strongly denounced, and at intervals everything pointed to the fact that a section of both houses were endeavouring to find a means whereby they could legally impeach the Chief Executive and expel him from his office.

Mr. Roosevelt was called a traitor to the cause of the white race ; while the negro as a people were roundly denounced by press and public.

Mr. Washington was grossly insulted on several occasions, and in divers manners, as a result of bitter feelings arising out of the same cause ; and isolated attacks were made upon members of the race throughout the country, as an aftermath of the Washington-Roosevelt incident.

There is no side-tracking the issue. The Americans, high and low, are bitterly opposed to the negro ; and they bluntly refuse to accord him that place which he has won, by virtue of his bravery, toil, or submission.

We have it in the American Civil War, where the negroes came forward and saved the North from the conquering South at a most trying moment, in the personal deed of valour on the battle-field, but of which there is scanty, if any, record in American history.

Negro troops saved Theodore Roosevelt at San Juan, and won the day for the United States; but the pen of the American historian has been quietly drawn across this event.

It was a negro who saved McKinley from immediate death by risking his own life in grappling with the assassin who was about to fire the third time upon the Chief Executive, while white men, whose duty it was to guard the president, fell back with the crowd.

The murderer was convicted and executed without the evidence of this man who saw it all; nor was he ever called to give information on the matter by any tribunal. His name was quietly left out of all proceedings connected with the event.

If Peary reached the North Pole, he did so by the aid of his able-bodied attendant, who saved his life on many occasions; but we have heard little of this negro since then, and less will be said of him by Peary of all persons, simply because of the opposition to the negro race.

Captain Bartlett, who did not reach the Pole, accompanied Lieutenant Peary on his lecture tour; but the man who stood beside him on the top of the world has been hurled back into the obscurity from which he came.

In these His Majesty's possessions we have no visible race-problem approaching in magnitude those which are found in the United States, and we do not want to create any by injudiciously inviting annexation to a power with whom it is impossible to live peaceably on any other terms than complete subserviency.

Do they (those who desire annexation) want to be told in their own country, when they knock at the accustomed door of God's House which had hitherto been opened to all comers : "You cannot come in here, this church has been reserved for white people only"?

The following is culled from the columns of the *Jamaica Gleaner*, written by Mr. H. G. De Lisser, its literary editor, which goes far in assisting to explain the incompatibility of the amalgamation as proposed by some.

"A Jamaica church-going crowd is of all classes and complexions, black and brown, and of all the intermediate hues.

"There is absolutely no attempt at separate churches for the different colours; such a thing would, I think, bring about a rebellion. There is no separating the congregation according to colour, and there can never be. I have been rather startled once or twice, upon entering a Jamaica church, to observe the darker members of the congregation, either sitting all to the back or to one side of the building.

"I have made inquiries. 'Those pews are rented at so much,' I was told, 'and those at so much, you see.' I saw.

"The division was based on solid financial grounds : it was cash, not colour, that made the difference, I observed.

"Nor is this supposition, for in this His Majesty's Island of Jamaica, everyone is abso-

lutely equal before the law, and knows it; and
where the population is chiefly coloured, no
church or other places of public or semi-public
nature, would think about colour discrimination.

" There also you find no unpleasant feeling
existing between the white and coloured population," etc.

A little further on in the same issue, the writer
goes on to say :

" The suburban life of the better classes in
Kingston bears points of similarity between
Jamaica and England, as far as the social customs
are concerned. In a hundred different ways you
will find the influence of England here, and of
English institutions.

" American manners and ideas are entering
into conflict with that influence, and it is hard
to say whether American or English example will
eventually prevail," etc.

In the first instance the editor touched upon
the religion of man and added his disapproval of
segregation in the church. He ventures to hint
on a possible rebellion, if such a course were to
be forced upon the West Indians as a people :
yet this is what the annexationist hopes to bring
to our doors, if their clamour for a union with
the United States is successful.

In the next paragraph he sustains me in my
contention that the West Indies have no colour
question of any moment to solve, in the broad
sense of the term ; and a little further on he
questioned the fact whether American or English

custom will ultimately prevail, owing to the present conflict of influence.

With reference to the suggestion as an alternative, that we be annexed to Canada, it must be borne in mind, that the people of the Dominion are not entirely different in sentiment from the people of the United States on the *race question*.

It is a common occurrence for East Indian and Japanese immigrants to be mobbed in Canada, and at times the situation has become so critical that military force has had to be summoned to quell the disturbances.

The negro in Canada is not exempted, and comes in for his share of outrage, notwithstanding that the strong arm of the law is always ready to protect every one ; but as the Dominion, like the United States, is essentially a white man's country, it is not possible to avert such eventualities.

Among the many instances of barbarous treatment of the coloured man in Canada in my recollection I shall mention this case : Not long ago, a coloured gentleman, after procuring a ticket at the box-office of a Toronto theatre, was refused admittance, and was told that " the management was not keen on negro patronage."

The individual in question insisted on his rights and was consequently forcibly ejected.

He appealed to the courts for redress in a suit of $500 and was awarded the full amount with costs ; but, notwithstanding that the plaintiff was successful in his suit, the moral effect was a signal one, since notice was thereby served on the public that the era for curtailing the privileges of the coloured man in Canada was at hand.

Quite recently (June 1910) two coloured students of medicine—British subjects from the Island of Trinidad—were refused admittance to a public anatomical show, held at Montreal, on account of their colour. They were kicked and beaten for no other reason than that they had the courage to go up to the ticket window and ask to be sold tickets for admission.

These instances amply suffice to illustrate, in the absence of any other, that the white people of the Dominion are no less drastic on the race problem than their American neighbours, the only difference between the two is, that your legal rights are recognized and treated impartially in the law courts of the former, while in the latter the negro has no legal status.

CHAPTER VIII

EXAMPLES OF AMERICAN RULE

AMONG the many vital questions which obstruct the annexation of the British West Indian possessions to the United States or Canada is that which has its origin in the subject of *race prejudice.*

Failure to give this most important point the amount of consideration which it justly deserves, before any change of sovereignty is contemplated, would be tantamount to selling a free, happy, and contented people into a form of perpetual slavery, from which there would be no means of escape, with the Yankees as our official masters.

Such a condition would, I am confident, bring about a state of anarchy culminating in consequences of such far-reaching magnitude as would require the attention and sympathy of the civilized world, when men, women, and children, with one accord, submit themselves to be butchered rather than be enslaved.

No annexation would be possible with such a giant problem unsolved ; for it would be impossible in such an event to safeguard the continued and uninterrupted happiness of a people, and as a favourable solution is impossible, there can be no affiliation.

No form of " treaty " could cover the question satisfactorily enough to be a lasting guarantee, and the only way to maintain their present relationship is to keep the two peoples in separate worlds as far as possible and permit them to have only a commercial intercourse.

Let the annexationists take a trip to Puerto Rico, Cuba, or the Philippines, and last, but not least, the Republic of Panama, and see for themselves how these people are being treated by the Americans, before attempting to barter their birthright for a mere shadow.

It is safe to say that the experience of the inquirer would be of such an astounding nature as to compel him to abandon his unrighteous cause for all time.

On the Isthmus of Panama, where, like the West Indies, the larger portion of the population is either mixed with negro or Indian blood, the expected has happened. Americans from the Canal Zone * who go over to the cities of Panama and Colon, on the territory of Panama, to make small purchases (the large purchases being procured from the U.S. Commissary) are now refusing to be attended to by coloured clerks, and as a result, managers and owners of these establishments have been contemplating whether, for the

---

* A strip of land ten miles wide, across the Isthmus of Panama acquired by the Americans for canal purposes.

benefit of their business, they should not dispense with coloured helps altogether.

There is great and widespread unrest in Cuba and Panama over the extreme position taken up by the Americans, who have assumed the position of official masters.

These people have made themselves overbearing in their manner to such an extent towards every one with whom they come in contact, that they foster hatred rather than love, to their discredit as juvenile colonizers.

The Republic of Panama, having practically surrendered their sovereignty to the United States in a most extraordinary document called the " Panama Canal Treaty," which gives the latter the *power of eminent domain in* perpetuity, are now in a quandary what to do with the Americans who have unblushingly taken unto themselves the rôle of dictators over their country.

It has come to this that obsolete canal officials, who are not quite up to canal acquirements, are being dumped on the defenceless Republic, at a salary next to that of its chief executive, and they dare not raise their voices in disapproval : so completely has their national dignity been forcibly put under.

Conditions at this moment do not represent a very comfortable aspect in the British West Indian Colonies under Crown Colony Government, but when all the circumstances are taken into consideration, we appear to be more comfortably

placed than Panama, which is to all appearances
an independent state.

To-day we are complaining, and justly so,
about the exorbitant salaries most of our officials
are receiving for their services, notwithstanding
that many of these colonies cannot turn over
enough revenue to pay their running expenses,
but comparing our position with that of Panama's,
it would certainly be adding *insult to injury* to
find ourselves called upon to contribute a salary
within £300 of that of the governor of Trinidad to
a cast-off engineer of the British Public Works
Department : yet this is the way things are done
at Panama.

No attempt is being made to infer that we are
free from outrages approaching those of our
neighbour across the Gulf ; on the contrary, as
the after pages of this book will show, we suffer
similar oppression from our official masters, the
only difference being that we, as a subjugated
people, have little or no say in these matters, and
therefore cannot help our position, while Panama,
as a Republic, ought to have everything to say
in such questions, but says nothing.

Our superior situation, therefore, appears to lie
in our defencelessness, and in the fact that in the
near future we hope to secure better conditions,
while the reverse seems to be the lot of our good
friend and neighbour the Republic of Panama.

Native families, that were bound together by
the most endearing and inseparable ties, are to
be found to-day estranged and driven apart,

since the advent of the Yankees with their pernicious colour question.

No sooner had the United States implanted herself on the Isthmus of Panama, than the Americans began to set up their *religion*, that the superiority of one man over the other was not dependent upon education, achievement, or wealth, but upon the hue of the skin.

At the restaurants and boarding-houses a screen would be put before the table of a previously welcomed coloured patron, and *that table* removed to the rear of the dining-room : then he would be asked to use the side entrance thereafter.

Since the advent of the Americans on the Isthmus, bar-rooms, ice-cream parlours, billiard parlours, and other places of refreshment and amusement which were opened to every one, now admit only white persons.

Those who travelled in Cuba returned with a tale of woe, that the same intolerable conditions exist there which were unknown in the darkest days of Spain's regime ; and the reason for this state of affairs is attributed to Yankee invasion.

It has been argued that the American Constitution does not follow the flag : that may be so, but it is a certainty that the feeling of race-hatred follows the people wherever they go.

Not many years ago, a few coloured American bishops had occasion to go to England to attend a convention. They engaged quarters at one of London's most fashionable hotels, where there were staying at the time other Americans (white), quite possibly belonging to what would be designated in the United States the better class of people.

The coloured bishops were no sooner installed in their new quarters than an indignation meeting was held among their white countrymen, with a view of ousting the new-comers as undesirables, and thus unfurl the red flag of *Yankee* prejudice in England.

At this conference it was unanimously decided that a delegation should be appointed to wait on the proprietor, and demand in the name of their white (American) patrons that the coloured bishops be forthwith expelled, basing the demand on the conclusion that such a thing would not be tolerated in the United States.

Naturally their terms, put forth in the style of a Yankee invasion of the British Isles, could not be accepted by a Britisher, so it was up to them to quit or stay. But it must not be understood that this stand was taken because the English love the negro best. No! It was the dictation of this foreign element which they did not like. Many of these white dignitaries chose the former course — that of quitting — threatening divers things about using their influence to prevent other Americans from patronizing this particular establishment ; but their threats were of no avail, since the tourist who does not elect to register at this particular hotel during his Continental tour, is supposed to be—*not in it*.

Somewhere, in one of London's most fashionable hostelries, is a manager or proprietor, who wears a gold watch and chain appropriately inscribed, *a gift of the coloured bishops*, as a tribute to his worthiness.

In some sections of the United States these exponents of the gospel might have been shot for a similar offence, and their bodies and belongings burnt as a public diversion, without any legal redress to their families, as no jury would be found in the " Land of the Free and the Home of the Brave," with the moral courage to convict white men for killing negroes.

The latest movement inaugurated against the coloured race in the United States, which number some seventeen million souls is to secure their wholesale deportation to a territory outside of the country. The organization, which has lodges throughout the Southern and in some of the Northern States, is called " The Order of True Americans," with headquarters at Rome, Georgia. Among its many peculiarities, this organization has that of being presided over by a minister of the gospel.

Where is this country *situated outside of the United States ?* Not Cuba, I am sure ! The American negroes could not live among and assimilate the ideas of the Cubans, which are distinctly Spanish. Not Hayti, I hope ! There the condition would be as bad, if not worse. Can it be that they hope to acquire the British West Indies for the carrying out of this scheme ?   This can be the only conclusion.   There the American negro would be welcomed, and there also would he find himself at home.

CHAPTER IX

LYNCH LAW AND THE FLAG

WOULD lynching follow the flag, if the British West Indian possessions are annexed to the United States ?

In order to settle the question as to whether lynch law would follow American occupation, it is necessary to determine whether the conditions which have brought forth this state of popular lawlessness in America are to be found in the West Indies.

If we take it to mean that such a state has been the natural consequence of the two opposite races in colour, having been brought together under one flag and in the same country as it is in the United States, then it should be admitted that the conditions really exist in the West Indies, even if in a lesser degree : but if we must assign another cause for the lawless assaults committed by one race upon the other in the former country, then the conditions do not exist in the West Indies.

It must be borne in mind, at the same time,

that much of this crime for which negroes are caught at first sight and lynched, is sometimes committed by white men, who, it is alleged, black their faces in order to escape legal punishment, in which they are oft-times successful. It cannot be stated positively the number of instances in which this has occurred, but that this ruse is said to have been largely practised leaves no room for doubt.

There are those who have advanced the theory that there will be no lynching in the West Indies if these islands happen to fall into the hands of the United States, and they submit as a basis for their argument, the occupation of Puerto Rico and the Philippines ; but they have purposely overlooked the fact that the American women,. the would-be subjects of these alleged attacks, as well as the class of men who do the lynching, are not much in evidence in these possessions.

It should not be understood that, if American women were very numerous in these islands, they would furnish subjects for assault upon their person ; but, as cases of lynching have been known to be meted out to persons of the coloured race for *offences* against these frocked angels, not amounting to assault, it is quite proper to say that their presence furnishes in most cases the causes for lynching.

The following is taken from *The Jamaica Gleaner* of June 25, 1910, under the heading of " Rule of Mobs " :

" I wish that you would please state that the lynching of Elmo Curl at Mastodon, Mississippi, was a most orderly affair, conducted by the bankers, lawyers, farmers, and merchants of that county.

" The best people of the country, as good as they are anywhere, simply met there and hanged Curl without a sign of rowdyism.

" There was no drinking, no shooting, no yelling, and not even any loud talking."

This was the statement which a well-dressed, nice-looking man who entered the Commercial Appeal Office yesterday afternoon asked to be published. He proved to be J. D. Miller, Tax Assessor of Concordia Parish, and brother of W. P. Miller, who was shot by Curl at Mastodon several weeks ago, when Mr. Miller went at the head of *a posse* to arrest him for *writing an insulting note to a white woman.*

It is a well-known fact that wherever the American (the entire Anglo-Saxon race for that matter) can exercise his freedom of action with women of alien races there is scarcely, if ever, any trouble ; but a decided state of restlessness develops when matters are reversed.

In this respect the white man seems to possess a special affinity for women of the negro race, with whom they beget illegitimate children, and thus bring into existence this " Third Race " problem—some of whom are legally without fathers or social standing among their father's kin.

This is the great problem which is stirring the white race throughout the civilized world into action, for they now find themselves confronted by the fruits of their own lawlessness—this " Third Race," which is clamouring for recognition in every walk of life that is pursued by their white sisters and brothers.

With the American people the question of this *new race* has presented itself in greater magnitude, from the fact that they are natives of the home of the white man, and must live and share his bread with him come what may.

They are forced by facts to admit that in the coming into being of this mixed-blooded type, the negro has played no active part, and that as far as these alien people are concerned, the standard of race purity has been, whether through forced circumstances or not, vigorously upheld by them. We are confronted by series of practical demonstrations that this *third race* have absolutely refused to identify themselves with their mother's sin (the black folk), even though they are cognizant of the fact that they can never hope to secure recognition of equality from those on their father's side.

As the irritation assumes alarming proportions we find the white races from every section of the globe who are guilty of this piracy upon morality, endeavouring to weld their sentiments together in order to find a solution ; but the great question before them is : What disposition can we make of these millions of discontented hybrids, the product of our outrages and imposition upon negro women, who are clamouring for the recognition which we, for the preservation of our own existence, cannot give ?

Where will it end ? No one knows. Will it be extermination, complete amalgamation, or a surrender on the part of the white race ? In the southern part of the United States, the coloured boys and girls are beginning to ask their negro mothers : " Where is my father ? Who is he ? " Then, and only then, is some white man, standing in the pulpit, before the Bar, on the Bench, or in the Legislative body, pointed out to him—they have all contributed to the making of this problem.

Those who have passed through more than one generation of intermixture with the whites are demanding a place in the *white circle*, with an utter disregard for all maternal feeling as far as her negro relatives are concerned, and notwithstanding their attainments—fair skin, blue eyes, and flowing golden hair, they fare no better than the blackest negro. They find to their dismay every avenue leading into the " white circle " barred against them because of their *one drop of negro blood*, and many prefer to return to the slavery which brought them into existence, rather than accept the inevitable, with the hope of finding an exit in complete amalgamation. The women will not marry a black man in most cases, because they imagine themselves white, a feeling in which no one else shares. The white man refuses to marry them from the fact that they are negroes ; and thus, labouring under their deplorable ignorance, many rather willingly submit themselves to all and every kind of indignity that the white man can possibly advance, rather than accept a negro as a lawful husband.

In the British West Indies or wherever the Englishman makes his home, temporarily or permanently, as far back as the days of slavery, when the negro slave woman would receive a command from her master, to " give Jane or Mary a good bath and send her up to the great house for the night," the negro race has been silently witnessing the debauching of their women.

Helpless and without a means of defence, the negro has meekly but sullenly witnessed the mixture of their blood with that of the white race, producing a degenerate type which is of no credit to either race, without being able to stem this tide of retrogression.

Who can say with a clear conscience that, even with superior advantages, the coloured man is the equal of the black, white, yellow, or pure-blooded of any race ?

I am taking it that all the races on earth did not spring from a single Adam and Eve, or a single creation.

Frail in constitution, he readily falls a prey to tuberculosis and other ravishing diseases : he is a subject of great weakness of mind, and companion of the most demoralizing vices. In these respects he stands out unique in his own narrow segregated sphere more an object of pity, *real pity*, than admiration.

These are in the main the illegitimate offspring of white men and negro women, whose mothers are the object of scorn and contempt in public and in social life, by those who are ever ready to pluck their virtues from them, satisfy their lust, and send them adrift.

Society will not ostracize them for their conduct, the church is ready to receive them with open arms ; the law will not intervene when the leading rôle is played by a member of the race which *now holds* the supreme position ; for they are the law makers and they make it to suit their convenience : hence there is no earthly help that will rescue the women of the downtrodden race from this state of perpetual slavery. We can only hope for justice at the hands of the Almighty against those who oppress us.

Plainly enough this seems to be the reward which the negro is receiving for the ancient and grand civilization which he has handed down to the now dominant race.

The following is quoted from Hall Caine's *Cruise of the Port Kingston* :

" It puzzles me to understand how the negro has been found so unworthy of study when our need of his service has been so urgent. Greek and Latin literature abounds with tributes to the beauty no less than the strength and fidelity of the race.

" It was in Ethiopia that the Jews were saved from extinction. Moses was born and educated in Ethiopia, and among her daughters found a wife.

" It was upon a negro the cross of Christ was laid that he might bear it after him to Calvary.

" The Ethiopian with his black skin and frizzled hair is still the object of contemporary curiosity and admiration, ' most just of men,' favourite of the gods.

" The historian of vision and caution finds him in the early days in the highest rank of knowledge and civilization, to whom, despite our present contempt (an interesting subject of reflection), we owe our *arts*, *science*, and even the very *speech* we use."

In bidding adieu to the subject, this greatest historian of modern times draws our attention to a verse in the Roman Catholic prayers, which refers to the Holy Virgin as black and beautiful, viz., " *Nigra sum sed formosa, filiæ Jerusalem,*" which is interpreted to mean that the mother of Jesus Christ was black of skin.

It would never do, for the supremacy of the white race, that they should acknowledge in too conspicuous a manner, or preach that the *Holy Virgin* was of negro blood : nor would it be considered consistent with their views to have the statue of the Virgin painted black instead of white. No ! It would be an outrage with but one exception, and that is to be found in the statue of the *Black Virgin* in the Chapel of St. Thomas of Ville Neuve, Paris.

The white race would rather turn Hebrew and side with the Jews in watching for the Messiah yet to come, than accept One who must naturally (if we do not read history with our eyes closed) have had negro blood in His veins. If substantial backing of the theory were to be discovered and disclosed, then good-bye to the religion of Christ the crucified so far as the white race are concerned.

With all this glorious history and tradition behind the black man, it is looked upon as a crime (though he does an injustice to his race) if he takes the hand of a white woman in marriage. This offence in some parts of the world is punishable with imprisonment.

In the *Cruise of the Port Kingston*, Hall Caine decries and brands it as an unpardonable offence for a black man to be permitted to link himself with a woman of the Caucasian race.

He says : " Every white woman of pure mind and of any knowledge of the simple elements of psychology shrinks from that touch of unholy contagion." Of course that is when the black man touches the *white woman* ; but he does not, in all fairness to the great question, complain when the white man compromises the black woman. Failing to deal with both sides, his readers are left to infer that *contagion* is only possible when the black man is the aggressor.

He is horrified at the very thought when the negro assumes the superior position as husband, but he overlooks the fact that in these marriages, unjustifiable as they are on either side to every well-thinking human being, it is the white woman who gains, and the black man loses. This is so since it is always the negro of fine breeding, wealth, and culture, that seeks to marry—not the white woman of similar attainments, or of modest lowly life in most cases, but some maid-in-waiting, scrub-girl, or restaurant waitress, an act which after a while fills him with regrets.

In such cases who wins ? The white servant-girl, of course ! And why ? Because she has been elevated to a position of which she had never dreamt, through the folly on the part of her black master.

Up to the present time, the only opposition shown by the English people against intermarriages, is the condemnation of the practice in almost every book written by Englishmen on the West Indies, and on the negro problem ; but in spite of these the two races continue to exercise their freedom of action in this respect, and intermarriages continue. They (the English people) have never gone beyond this, nor has there been any attempt to legislate against either race in the exercise of their private prerogative, nor can they afford to enact special legislation to that end, having regard for the large numbers of negroes under their control : yet the world is fast becoming Americanized, and England is no exception.

To-day we have in that great metropolis, London, many a public place where a black man will be politely told : " No room, all occupied."

Some say that this is the outcome of the continued agitation on one side by the American in London, and on the other, the greed for the Yankee dollar by the English. Things are really not what they used to be.

CHAPTER X

THE POLICY OF THE AMERICANS

SPAIN did not pave the way in her colonies for the English-speaking nations, and that explains the reason why the natives of Puerto Rico and the Philippines have not been, as yet, crowded out of existence, in every walk of life, by their new owners.

With the acquisition of British West Indian possessions, however, matters would soon assume a different aspect and the fight to drive the native population into the background would begin immediately, without any effort to assimilate local custom and manners.

Means would be readily devised to strangle the business capacity of our coloured merchants, and thus finally oust them from the arena of mercantile combat.

Our white merchants, some of whom are at present clamouring for annexation, would be forced to make way for gigantic combinations with which they would find it impossible to compete, and the final result would be the wiping out of our native West Indian commercial men of the present day.

Our present office-holders would be dropped and men imported from the United States to fill their places ; thus forcing the natives to migrate, or to accept such offices as even a *coolie* would scorn.

There could be no meeting the proposition half-way. Every man behind the provision or dry-goods counter ; clerks of the government offices ; their assistants, such as revenue clerks ; Post Office clerks, etc., would be an American or, at least, a white man.

It would be found impossible to cultivate the friendship of this people whose idea of the superiority of one race over the other is not subject to modification ; and whose sole object is to subjugate all coloured races, rather than take them by the hand along the brotherly walks of life.

We should speak of the American without any thought of his being a part of the Anglo-Saxon race, as it appears that within the last century a new race of people has been produced in the United States.

It will be observed that extensive immigration and intermixture of the different nationalities, have brought forth a distinct type to that resulting from a mixture of the Angles and the Saxons.

Savage, lacking restraint, more of the excitable Spaniard than the slow-moving methodical Briton, quick to destroy the life of his fellow men, he shows the traits of the Italian. Boastful, and ever ready to proclaim his own achievements, he shows the

Dutch that is in him. These blended with the characteristics of German, French, Spanish, and of every other known nationality which stands out prominently here and there, we have before us an entirely distinct race of people.

The difference between the acknowledged Anglo-Saxon and the American in temperament as well as in habit is so conspicuous that it would, in my opinion, be safe to term them the new race of people. In their system of colonization they have wantonly put to the sword all that opposed them, whether in peace or war.

Ask the average American what has become of the millions of red men that thronged the Northern portion of the American continent from the ever-glades of Florida to the borders of Lake Champlain.

He will tell you, with a wave of the hand, that this grand and noble race of free-men, with whom the early Britons made friends, have succumbed to the *white man's* civilization : a civilization of whisky, vice, shots, and shells.

Go to India and see the advanced stage through which the natives are passing under British rule, and compare it with the advance of the red men under Yankee tutelage, and you will at once see that the British, with all their faults—and they are legion—are the best colonizers of the present age.

You will find the Indians emancipated from the wife-burning fad, filling magisterial and other positions of trust ; as members of the viceregal council ; and to-day we hear talk of an Indian constitution in the near future.

The progress of these people under British rule, and the keeping intact of the race with all their ancient rights in so far as they were consistent with the present-day civilization, would have been one of England's most glorious achievements, had it not been allowed to become tainted by the *Slave Trade* among the natives ; and in other words, the exportation of the people, like so many oxen, to foreign lands for a *specific time* and a *specific purpose*, with all the accompanying disadvantages.

Notwithstanding this terrible blot upon Britain's Indian administration, these people have never been persecuted to the limit of extermination ; or called upon to share the fate of the American Indians, who, hunted and hounded, are finally driven to the remote fastness of what was once their country ; hemmed in on every side by soldiers, discriminated against and discriminated down to the insignificant figure of 300,000 souls, all told.

Men of undoubted wisdom have said in plain language, that the East Indians would fare no better had the English elected to colonize India and make it the home of the white man, but that is a charge which cannot be borne out by facts.

It is plain, therefore, that the policy of the Americans towards alien races, is to force them into a submission bordering on slavery, or extermination.

This is precisely the condition which those who, under annexation, refuse to be completely subjugated by their new masters would be called upon to face.

With the advent of this people, the small man in our industrial life would be forced out of existence, before the octopus trust and other formidable combinations so common to American business life.

It would be useless to complain or to point out the injustice done to the middle man by the existence of these organizations, for the complainant would be very promptly told that the constitution does not follow the flag.

The clerk contingent which is at present recruited from among our native gentlefolk—men and women—without distinction of colour or race, would also be made to give way to importations from the States ; and those who survive the ordeal would be made to feel their inferiority by having placed under them men whom they would have to teach the routine of the business, but who would receive twice as much pay as themselves. This is what has been done on the Canal Zone.

In the West Indies, most of those employed behind the counter and desks are recruited from the coloured section of the population. This is in direct contrast with the custom in the United States, where it would mean death to an employer's business were he to engage the services of any but *white persons*.

The coloured physician who practises his profession in the country towns of the *South* will tell you that he is permitted to do so at the will of the white people. If they say " That's a good nigger," then he might stay and labour among such of his own people as white physicians do not care to treat.

The coloured lawyers who practise before the Police Court in the large cities, as well as in the country towns, will tell you that the *Courts* are not favourable towards them ; and in consequence they are obliged to seek their living by accepting such cases as white lawyers not do care to handle, carrying fees ranging from twenty-five cents to a dollar or two.

These are but a few of the evils that would come with annexation of the British West Indian possessions to the United States of America.

Does the annexationist desire to bring about this intolerable state of affairs in the only spot of earth where persons of the negro race have a chance of existence ?

Do they, the annexationists, want to be told in their hotels, restaurants, saloons, theatres, churches, parks, and other places now at the disposal of the public, that their presence is not wanted because of their colour ?

Do they desire to see the day when our railway trains must by law carry separate cars for white and coloured people, with the former having all the comforts, while the latter is divested of all, even though they must pay the same rate of mileage ?

Do they—the annexationists—want to see the day when separation of the races on the street cars (trams) becomes the order : the coloured folk of all grades, caste, and classes, sitting to the rear, with their faces turned to the opposite direction to that in which the car is going ?

Do they fully realize that under the American flag coloured persons owning property in prominent localities, would be forced, *without exception*, under threats to sell their property to white people and retire to the negro section (a part set aside for the habitation of those having negro blood) ?

In short, do they want to be ruthlessly divested of every symbol of right which they now possess and enjoy ? If so, then let it be annexation by all means, as that would be the surest and most ready way of ridding themselves of the benefits which they are, up to the present, enjoying without intimidation or molestation in any shape or form.

The agitators should bear in mind that the British West Indian possessions are, by the most sacred rights, the assets of the coloured man—a product of the part which the British Government played in the slave trade in connection with her possessions in the Western Hemisphere.

This mixed race cannot return to Africa, the home of their fore-parents even if they so desired, as Africa does not want them. They could not safely migrate to England in considerable numbers, carrying with them their cares and necessities, as this course would cause intense excitement in the British Isles : such a proposition would not be countenanced for a single moment by the British public.

The English people for the most part know the colour question only as they find it in the tropics, where every Englishman is a miniature king or czar in himself ; and they have the privilege of being able to leave it where they found it, in that they have no special reason to emit venom at the mere mention of a few coloured people in London or in Edinburgh ; but they certainly would rise up in arms and exterminate this foreign element, if three million negroes were to be turned loose in their cities, seeking for bread and claiming equal rights as British subjects. Why, they would be driven into the Thames, lock, stock, and barrel, there to feed the fishes with their bodies.

In such a case it would be hard to choose between Briton and Yankee, as to which is the more humane master ; and it is a pre-concluded fact—should the occasion arise—that the verdict would be returned in favour of the Yankee. The American white man knows the negro, as they are associated with each other from infancy, and though the former hates the latter, he will permit him—even in considerable numbers—to live in the same country with himself : but in England any bulk of coloured people would be looked upon and treated as a foreign substance—something to be got rid of.

Such a position would be exceedingly difficult

and would most certainly, under such conditions, bring about unceasing conflicts, which would naturally result in the destruction of the weaker race. The English people would not stand for it ; it would not be tolerated in England or in any other European country.

The Briton in the West Indies differs from the Yankee in the States, in that being always placed in a superior position to that of the average native, he does not have him as a direct competitor, hence he dislikes the negro only because he is black. With the Yankee the matter assumes quite a different aspect. Competition at home makes him regard the negro as a force to be combated, and consequently he endeavours to displace him in every avenue where he threatens the supremacy of the white race.

This is made so from the fact that the United States is the home of 15,000,000 negroes, while Great Britain is free from a negro population and its consequent problem.

The policy of the Americans is to attack and disarm the negro of the implements with which he must fight his way through life, and to relegate him forcibly (speaking of the general whole) to a position of inferiority, where he is no longer a menace to the sovereignty of the white race.

What then would become of the negro of the British West Indies, if he and his possessions be sold for a price, as some of the gods would suggest, to our giant neighbour ?

The future for such a people is clouded with

dread possibilities. Seeing the *end* approaching we must unite in seeking to protect the land of our birth, a land rich by the labours of our fore-fathers ; a land saturated with the blood that ran from the negroes' wounds at each scourge of the whip of their masters, as they toiled in pain and woe.

Our white population could migrate, if conditions did not suit them in the change of authority which seems inevitable (if something is not done to " stem the tide "), and be lost in the crowd of any of the large cities of Europe. But the negro with the mark of " Ham " could never hope to escape detection, if he adopted a similar course, and the wrath that must necessarily follow ; his home, therefore, is in the land of his nativity, which is his only refuge.

The British West Indies have no race issue of any moment to solve. This is chiefly due to the fact that these islands are not the home of the white man. There are no prospects of any grave question on the subject arising at this late day under the present form of administration.

The people of all classes, natives and sojourners, have learned to love and trust one another, and they naturally look with disfavour upon any propaganda whose object is to agitate the race problem.

There are some who speak in high terms of the extra capital that would be invested in these possessions by American capitalists if they were annexed to the United States : of this there is no doubt. There are others who, having designs upon American society, as a social gain, are willing to risk this new adventure for purely personal gains ; but these evidently have not reckoned with their hosts.

I do not doubt for one moment that extra capital from American sources would flow into these colonies once they are placed under the ban of the Stars and Stripes : but it must be remembered that the native West Indian would be a very little benefited, if at all, since any great influx of money would be controlled by large combinations, which would put an end to the middle man in our commercial sphere.

As regards the extra labour that would be employed in conjunction therewith, such would most assuredly be brought in from abroad.

The Yankee, with his inborn hatred for persons of the negro race, would import with the taxpayer's money white immigrants from Southern Spain and Italy, and pay them two or three times the rate offered for native labour, and thus bring about conditions 100 per cent. worse than those of which we are now complaining—in respect to the importation of East Indian coolies.

The American method of colonial administration conveys, even to the casual observer, stern and forcible object-lessons from which one may gather many a painful but valuable experience.

Strange as it may seem, yet it is true that notwithstanding the enormous external trade of Puerto Rico which has, since the American occupation, risen from fifteen to twenty million dollars, and which ought to be considered sufficient prosperity for such a short period, to make a people happy, contented, and buoyant with hope; yet the contrary exists.

Where we should naturally look for rejoicing on all sides, we find dissatisfaction, restlessness, and an intense and growing hatred for their official masters.   Where we should have a gala day, hear music, and see a city decorated with bunting and flags for the reception of an incoming American governor, we find in place of decorations or merry-making, flags at half-mast, draped in mourning.   Why is this so?   Because the native Puerto Rican finds himself ousted from all these avenues that were opened to him during Spain's regime, bad as that was.

The Americans have stopped at nothing.   They have gone to the extent of importing elementary teachers from the United States to take the place of the native ones, thus reducing their scope for earning a livelihood.   The islanders, finding their liberty thus narrowed and circumscribed, have become callous, and care little for the rest of what is going on or is being attempted on behalf of the islands.

Let the annexationist be mindful that liberty, even such as Spain gave to her colonies, is voluminous in comparison with that which is meted out by the Americans to their colonial possessions.

We should, therefore, cherish that scope of freedom of action which we now enjoy (even under a *Crown System of Government*, which is certainly not the best form of administration for civilized man) as a priceless gift, until the tables turn in our favour.

For liberty, men have sacrificed their lives and their all ; and there are millions ready to-day to go to their death for its preservation : this is the price put upon this great gift of God to mankind.

The inhabitants of Puertó Rico, Cuba, and Panama, would gladly return to their former control, rather than tolerate for another day the dictates which come with American rule, but it is *too late! too late!!* The one is tied down by the laws governing the conquest of territory, and the other by a Treaty which runs in perpetuity, while Cuba occupies a position of uncertainty, liable to be pounced down upon at any moment.

Never since the annals of history has a conquering race been more distasteful to the conquered than this new people, who are afflicted with the nightmare that they are the superior of all mortals.

The object-lesson has been set plainly enough for us to be forewarned of what fruits the future must necessarily bring. Are we to be benefited by what we have seen with our eyes and realized by our senses ; or shall we close our eyes to the danger, and our ears to the bragging words of these Yankees—" We have got Puerto Rico and Cuba, and we will get Jamaica and the rest soon "—and step into the chasm and be lost for ever ?

Such an utterance coming from a people who have the means at hand to make their word good, is a subject worthy of the gravest deliberation by every West Indian, at home or abroad.

CHAPTER XI

AMERICAN JUSTICE ONE OF POLITICS AND COLOUR

THE administration of justice, in most cases, as it is dispensed by the American courts, both at home and in her colonies, is based upon political standing and colour.

Judges hold their appointments by virtue of their politics, and the law is dispensed accordingly.

It is almost invariably insinuated that in the United States *politics* and *graft* go hand in hand. And this is true to some extent in most countries, where the administration of justice finds itself inseparable from these conditions, thereby creating an uncomfortable position for the masses.

Strange and incomprehensible as it may seem to those who have been brought up under British rule, yet it is nevertheless true that the colour of a prisoner at the bar of an American Court of Justice decides his fate, in many instances, before his cause is heard.

American jurors have placed it on record that, in an issue where a white man is accused of the murder of a negro, they would not return a verdict in favour of the dead man, no matter what the evidence might prove.

Negroes have been shot down without provocation and otherwise foully murdered, in the United States and in its colonial possessions, by white men, but the murderers have yet to pay the legal penalty for these outrages : because neither judge, jury, nor public, is in favour of equal rights for the negro before the law, or in any other station of life.

In the Drede-Scott case before the Supreme Court of the United States, it was decided that the negro has no rights which the white man is bound to respect.

At no time, in an American court of justice, is the representation of a coloured man taken seriously when made in opposition to the interest of a white man. Whatever may be the drawbacks, due to the present form of government, which we are called upon to face, there is one thing that gives satisfaction to the mind, and that is, our laws are administered without fear or favour.

The British flag is an emblem of equal rights *before the law*, for every citizen or subject, in which foreigners from the remotest part of the globe share and share alike.

British justice knows no politics, no creed, no colour, no fear, no favour. It does not regard wealth, present or past standing of those who are brought under its ban : hence, every one

has implicit faith in the majesty of British law
—that justice will be administered without par-
tiality.

This is something which the American, high
and low, cannot understand. For the very reason
of the difference of the administration of the law
in the two countries, the people of the United
States could not understand why Mrs. Florence
Maybrick, the daughter of a former Alabama
banker, a woman of wealth and refinement, should
have been held for so many years in a British
criminal prison for the killing of her husband,
James Maybrick, an Englishman, with arsenic
obtained by soaking fly-papers in water with
which she cooked his gruel.

In the same way, the English people could not
comprehend the lengthy agitation which was
carried on in the United States during the in-
carceration of this woman, nor could they understand the part played by the American Government directed from Washington, which in all
respects seemed to have charged every American
ambassador to the Court of St. James's with the
commission of securing her release.

To have sent a woman of Mrs. Maybrick's
position and social standing to prison in the
United States would have taxed the energies of
the Government to their last extremities, only to
result in ignominious failure.

Prison in the land of " Dementia Americana "
was not made for such creatures.

In England, or wherever British rule is supreme,

things are different : there her position, wealth, and social standing were fully recognized, but they had no bearing upon the law or those who are charged with its administration. The offence was treated as an everyday criminal occurrence, unworthy of any particular notice or comment, save for the ingenuity which woman wit had infused in the accomplishment of the dastardly crime.

Had James Maybrick been murdered in America, Florence Maybrick his wife, the convicted murderess, would never have been brought to trial.

The circumstances attendant on the effort to secure the release of this woman from prison evidence the fact that the same politics in American life which ought to, and ultimately did, succeed in obtaining the freedom of this woman would, in all probability, have prevented her from suffering any form of imprisonment, had the crime been committed in the United States instead of in England.

British subjects have something to reverence, and that is the *Majesty of British Law*. It is the source of protection of our crowned heads, religion, life, limb, and property, throughout the United Empire. It protects the persecuted of any country who land upon British soil. Its impartial administration has sheathed the dagger of the anarchist, and affords him shelter when all the world oppress him. In England, the black-hand with his blood-stained weapon takes on the garb of a citizen, and he is as harmless as a lamb. His strength is in the Law.

CHAPTER XII

SOCIAL ENEMY BUT COMMERCIAL FRIEND

FOREMOST in our commercial life, not excepting Britain, stands the great American Republic—the United States of America.

It is to her markets that we look chiefly for the disposal of our products. In every nook of the British West Indian possessions we find the American trader firmly implanted.

He has been the beacon light of our prosperity and regeneration when, beset by storms, earthquakes, and hurricanes, we tottered as if about to fall, and in all probability would have fallen, were it not for the inexhaustible ability of this great country to give and take of the world's produce.

Regrettable as it may seem for a British subject to admit, on behalf of a colony like Jamaica, that were it not for American markets, and American capital for the most part, that island would have long ceased to be of any more importance in the world's history than a stranded iceberg.

In fifty years, the important matter of railroad transportation, under governmental supervision, did not advance more than fifty miles to any appreciable degree ; but with American capital and energy, within five years that island was a network of railroad lines, and so it is with a good many of the improvements in other parts of the West Indies.

In these days we read much of a direct line, with its divergent objects, from the mother country to the West Indies ; of the strenuous efforts that Canada is making along similar lines. Much is said of our chances to send our banana, sugar, cocoa, and other tropical products to the markets of these countries, for which we are justly proud, even though these helping hands are somewhat late in coming.

American capital has been the upkeep of the fruit trade of the West Indies, from distant Guiana to Jamaica, and were it not for Yankee energy, there would have been little or no fruit to ship to England or Canada, and precious little of other products.

These British West Indian possessions owe the United States everlasting gratitude, no matter what future glories await them in British and Canadian markets, for the ever-ready assistance so cheerfully extended to these colonies in their gloomiest hours, when no other help seemed nigh.

However, despite the gross neglect of the mother country to her West Indian colonies and subjects generally, we love her still, since, rightly or wrongly, she is our mother country, and no one can take the place of mother in all things.

Between the years 1899 and 1900 the United

States took no less than thirty million dollars of the total export of the British West Indian colonies, and sent us during the same period over thirty-three million dollars in food stuffs and other staple articles. To-day we find that we are importing maize (Indian corn) to the extent of one million dollars annually from her.

For the financial year ended June 30, 1908, we also find that our neighbour has imported from these colonies an amount in excess of twelve million dollars, and exported to us nearly fourteen million dollars in food stuffs and other commodities : an exchange, when figures are computed, which we accept as favourable, notwithstanding that we are placed on the debit side of the balance sheet.

In the same year Great Britain sent us a little over two and three-quarter million pounds sterling and took from us three million pounds sterling in fruits and other tropical products out of a total export trade of over ten (10) million pounds sterling : the difference in our export going to foreign countries, with a portion to Canada.

It will thus be seen that, for the want of preferential treatment in the markets of the mother country, a large portion of our products, which should have found its way into the English markets, was sent to the United States, and, notwithstanding that we found ourselves compelled to pay her something nearing half a *million pounds* sterling in cash—that being the difference of our accounts, she having sent us that much in excess of what she took—until better arrangements can be made one way or the other, there seems to be no remedy for the situation.

During the same period we find for Canada's financial year that she sent us three and a half million dollars of Canadian products while she took from us in return something slightly in excess of *nine million dollars* out of a total export trade of ten million pounds sterling. In this particular, allowing for all discrepancies in figures, it appears that over one million pounds sterling came out of the pockets of the Canadian consumers, and went into those of the West Indian producers, to satisfy the difference in account ; a state of affairs which is indeed very promising for us, looking at the situation from a protective point of view.

It appears, however, that inasmuch as we can boast of the glorious prospects for trade with Canada, although still in its embryonic state, we should not be too precipitate in our action, since her capacity to consume tropical products is still small, and she has plenty to sell ; and, consequently, if given preference, would in a short time convert these colonies into a veritable dumping ground, throwing us into a state of chronic bankruptcy if she were our sole dependence.

Luckily we still have the markets of the United States open to us, to dispose of that surplus which finds its way neither to British nor Canadian markets.

If we were self-governing colonies under confederacy, it would most likely be to our own interest to seek at once to enter into a commercial agreement with the United States, before it is too late ; but under *Crown Colony Government* we are denied that privilege, and must therefore stand with folded arms, looking on helplessly, until the products in which we now claim pre-eminence are fully developed in her tropical possessions and dependencies, only to find ourselves left hopelessly in the rear and " out in the cold " for the most part.

The aggregate surface area of British possessions in the Western Hemisphere is about three times that of the Island of Cuba. But, in spite of our bulk, she has fairly put us to shame in the development of her resources and the management generally of her affairs.

With a population of about $1\frac{1}{2}$ million she has managed, during the past eight years, to show an appreciable balance to her credit at the end of each financial year, and great things are promised for 1912.

In the year 1905 her exports were *two million pounds sterling* more than her imports, which means that amount of outside cash was paid into the hands of the Cuban producers to the benefit of the island—a very good lesson in political economy.

As soon as the people of the United States find themselves well supplied with the tropical necessities from their own colonies, which they now get mainly from neighbouring British possessions, there will surely come a change in their attitude towards us. It will then be annexation by all means, or starvation, unless we can find another outlet for our products.

If when this inevitable change comes it finds us armed with a commercial treaty, there might be some hope still, if for no more than during the life of the agreement ; for with bananas, cocoa, coco-nuts, oranges, etc., going into her markets, in sufficient quantities from Cuba, Puerto Rico, and the Canal Zone, under preferential treatment, then good-bye to her trade with the British West Indian possessions.

By withdrawing her patronage from us to her own field of direct influence, she would use her strong financial position as a lever to force annexation, for while she takes little or nothing from us we should still find the necessity of going to her markets for supplies in food stuffs, owing to the inducement which she would be able to offer us, and thus find ourselves each year more and more her debtor, without an opportunity of liquidating this debt in a manner beneficial to ourselves.

For, seeing the breakers ahead, directly in our path, we begin to seek an alternative course before our bark is wrecked upon the shoals of annexation at all hazards, or complete bankruptcy. We ask in our dilemma, When will Canada ever be in a position to take the place which her great rival has so worthily filled in British West Indies ?

Let us hope earnestly that she will soon be able ; but at this moment, were the issue to fall upon her with a comparatively speaking small population of but five million inhabitants, she would be entirely out of the race.

It will be twenty-five years yet, before her population, under immigration, shall have increased to such an extent as to place her in a position to stand by us when the crisis comes.

That the future of the Dominion is great beyond all imagination is too true, and so sanguine are the Canadians of their future greatness that it is a subject of constant amusement among her more ambitious politicians, whether they should not begin to lay plans for the annexation of their big neighbour, the United States.

In whatever upward move she may make, she carries with it the very best wishes of the British West Indian colonies, and that appears as far as we can go for the present, in justice to our frail position in the financial and commercial world. All in all (setting aside race prejudice and other national traits which do not appeal to the average West Indian, who has been brought up under British rule as equitable), we must, in justice to a fair conscience, agree that the United States is, commercially speaking, the best friend we have.

Besides taking a large bulk of our products (many of which are admitted *free of duty*), supplying us with food, ready to aid in times of disaster, she has kept the island of Jamaica and its dependencies from bankruptcy, and consequently its inhabitants from starvation, by its capital invested in the island and in the neighbouring republics, by which *all the West Indies* have been to a small or great extent benefited.

Can we call her, in spite of other differences, less than *friend* ?

CHAPTER XIII

OUR RELATIONS WITH CANADA

In view of the fact that America, baffled in her scheme of annexation by the timely infusion of practical *self-government* by Great Britain among her colonies in the West Indies under federation, would in all probability begin a series of retaliating tactics, by tariffs and other means, we must prepare to face the position.

There are some who argue that the British West Indian possessions, federated with responsible government, would see the dawn of an era of great friendship between the United West Indies and the United States of America ; but in the face of no direct guarantee of such an outcome, I take it that if, in such an event, she wishes to crush us by closing her markets to our products, Canada offers the only refuge.

It is therefore to our interest to begin at once to cultivate a market in the Dominion, as an outlet for our export, and to do all that is in our power to bring about the best understanding along commercial lines ; but we should be careful not to attempt to discriminate against the United States, or to give her any affront that might cause unpleasantness and our undoing, by being too premature.

True enough, distance, aided by rigid winters, offers tremendous barriers at first sight to our commercial relations with Canada; but in these days of fast transportation, at least one of the main obstacles has been overcome.

The great question before us, in connection with the development of our trade with Canada, is: whether we should grant a subsidy to her merchant ships plying between West Indian Ports and those of the Dominion.

It appears that the majority of those who are directly concerned in the welfare of these colonies do not favour such a course, and it is argued that it would be detrimental to our best interest, since it would tend to create a monopoly by shutting off outside competition, and the consequent maintenance of a high freight rate to our own sorrow.

Another grave question in this connection is: Should we grant preference to goods coming from Canada into the West Indies? No! emphatically No! We have too much to lose in running such a risk.

Let us take the case of a colony like Jamaica as an example. It would be a suicidal policy for her to attempt such a thing, having regard for her present relations with the United States, and this is true, for the most part, of other British colonies in the West Indies.

It has been hinted that there are a few of the colonies that could safely, and are willing to, lean on Canada for their all, to take and to give. But it would be considerably more beneficial if the British West Indies would stand together as a unit on the matter of preferential treatment or subsidy to the Dominion.

This division of petty sentiments in the West Indies on questions of vital interest to all the possessions is a weakness, and is in itself sufficient proof that *federation* would be the best state for us. It should be one for all and all for one in spirit as well as in practice, instead of attempting to work out our destiny individually, as if we were so many independent states. This system cannot but result in dismal failure, owing to the poverty-stricken condition of some of these islands.

What appears to be most urgently necessary for the West Indies is an equalization of their *wealth* as well as their burden. This can only be so, if they are confederated under one head, thus removing all petty restrictions to free immigration among the colonies, and the opening up of inter-colonial free trade.

It is given out by the West Indian Committee circular dated March 15, 1910 :

" That the evidence given before the commission on trade relations between Canada and the West Indies has made it clear that those colonies whose products, such as cocoa and banana, is ' unlikely ' to be consumed in any quantities in Canada for some considerable time to come would nevertheless be willing to enter into a preference trade agreement with the Dominion."

The above statement shows on its face that the parties who gave such evidence before the committee have little or no cocoa or banana to sell in any market, as such a proposition would be decidedly against their own interest.

In such a case it is plain that those islands which grow cocoa and banana, and are willing to give preference to Canada, discriminating against the United States, with the full knowledge that the Dominion would not be able, for some *considerable* time, to consume any great quantities of their products, are playing a losing game, in which they must make powerful enemies.

We who are familiar with the *one-horse* policy on which the government of these West Indies is run, can promptly denounce such a statement as treacherous and in diametrical opposition to the wishes of the people—the disfranchised tax-payers.

Such a statement as contained in the *Circular* quoted might well have come from a dry goods merchant, whose desire would be to have Canadian manufactured goods admitted into these colonies free of duty, if possible, for his personal gain; but one would hardly conclude that there is a cocoa or a banana planter who is so dead to his own interest as to have put forward such a sacrificial suggestion.

We know as a fact, and it is a matter of record, that in no question appertaining to the welfare of the West Indies the wishes of the masses— those whose particular interests are mostly at stake—are ever consulted. The whole affair is handled by the local colonial office on one hand, and a few *shopkeepers* and *slave owners* (men who employ coolie labour for specific time and purpose) on the other hand : thus is constituted the official advisers of the Home Office.

In this connection we are no better off than *darkest* Russia, with Colonial Office at Downing Street as the *Duma*, and the Secretary of State for the Colonies as our Czar—the only difference being that, as we are separated by a broad expanse of water, *our Czar* has not the necessity to be guarded night and day by faithful soldiers, or finds himself occasionally exiled in his office. All West Indians who are interested in the welfare of these colonies know that the history of the Colonial Office in this connection has been a long series of the most deplorable blunders, one after the other, in its effort to place the remnant over the bulk, or, in other words, to establish and maintain at all costs the minority over the majority.

" The Royal Commission " thought that they fell into a bed of roses on their whirlwind tour. They thought that they had heard representatives from all the people ; but we who are on the ground laughed heartily at the fact that these men, with great titles and classic education, allowed themselves to be so completely duped.

The thing was cut and dried, by the *few chosen*, long before these noblemen set foot on West Indian soil (I refer to those Islands that have all to lose through favouring preference to Canada) ; and the people who have all to lose, although possessing no voice in the management of the affairs of Government, were seriously amused at the fraud perpetrated on the learned Commission.

In one instance, to the knowledge of many persons in a certain colony, the meeting of the Commission took place in the hall set apart for the use of the Legislative Council of the island.

The first person called upon to give evidence was an official of the Government, a collector of customs, and before he had concluded his testimony the local colonial secretary was busy despatching a cable to the Home Office, intimating that *that particular Colony* was favourable to granting preference to the Dominion. A complete case of " frame up."

Such is the precious evidence which the " Commission " has gathered in the *favourable Islands*, and it fully demonstrates how the wishes of the people are ascertained in a British Crown Colony ; and from this single act of *kidnapping the Commission*, the true value of the bulk of evidence gathered in these parts by this august body can be fairly estimated.

The West Indian Committee goes on to say in the afore-mentioned *circular* that there are no real grounds for fearing hostile treatment from the United States, for, after all, the West Indies would only be seeking to do what America is already doing with her own dependencies.

It would be a great relief if we could be satisfied

that the United States would stand passively and see the West Indies actually close their markets against her products, in favour of the same articles coming from Canada, and still allow these colonies to use her markets to dispose of their products without protest.

The West Indian committee certainly does not give the Americans credit for being able to protect their own interest, and we are apt to be mightily fooled if we unwittingly put any reliance on the theories evolved by this *little body*.

It is true that Lord Balfour of Burleigh interviewed President Taft, as well as other high American officials in a position to judge, who gave him their assurances that there would be no retaliation from that country; but it must be borne in mind that the policies of governments are guided by the sentiments and feelings of other governments, who are directly interested in the issue under consideration, and as the question of self-preservation is always a subject of paramount importance to the American people, one can hardly rely on such assurances.

If we elect to be led by the West Indian Committee, the consequence of such a policy might be more far-reaching than most of us are willing honestly to forecast.

Did not England wage war on China because the latter sought to restrict the extensive opium trade which was being carried on between that country and India ?

Would not Germany for certainty wage war

against England the day she set up tariff barriers against her ?

These examples are based upon the same principles of discrimination which some of us are endeavouring to adopt, in spite of our senses and the dire consequences which are likely to follow.

Mr. Taft, or any other American official, could not for certain give assurance as to the course of events that would follow the granting of preference by the West Indies to Canada, and whatever he (Mr. Taft) may have told His Lordship cannot be taken as binding on the American people, who always pin their faith to the *almighty dollar.* America is a Republic.

We should, therefore, be taking a leap in the dark to show favours of the kind to the Dominion (preference), which would be a bad policy in any case, with our present knowledge that *our cocoa and banana* (the backbone of the West Indies thus far) are *unlikely to be consumed in any quantities in Canada for a considerable time to come.*

Most certainly we should think well before we move, for once the hand is set to the plough there can be no looking back—it would be too late to recall a single act.

There is still another question which concerns every West Indian, and that is : Should we seek annexation to Canada, as some seem to favour, as a means of escaping Yankee domination ?

Again the answer seems to be unfavourable to such a course as an alternative. From all that can be gathered it appears that the adoption of this avenue of escape would certainly not lead us into the paradise for which we are yearning : on the contrary it would most likely bring about very unpleasant relationship where the feelings were otherwise of the best, and which could have been avoided by the exercise of a little forethought.

It must not be forgotten that Canada has her own *social* and *race* problem to solve, and has absolutely no desire to add to these.

The Dominion does not seek " political affiiliation," says the *Daily Witness*—a Montreal paper.

This paper expresses the hope that the Imperial movement of the Royal Commission does not look to " political affiliation."

It goes on to say :

" Perhaps this is in part a selfish wish, and a desire to escape the *white man's* burden, for surely Canada has enough race problems on her hands without adopting entirely new ones."

If we take the *Witness* as expressing the wish of the Canadian people, which I firmly believe it does, then the Dominion has made it very plain that she fears the *negro problem*, and she seeks to make no tie with the West Indies other than a purely commercial one.

She has thus sounded the death knell to the ambition of those who had hoped to see the British West Indian colonies annexed to Canada. The Dominion would not have these possessions, with their negro population, as a Christmas gift from *Santa Claus*.

Continuing the same paper goes on to say :

" Just as the acquisition of Alaska was offensive to Canada, and the acquisition of Greenland would be, so the annexation to the Dominion of these tropical islands would be offensive to the United States.

" The actual offence would be infinitely less, the circumstances as well as the proportion of things being infinitely different ; but as between the lamb and the wolf, a very minor cause may result in a very major offence.

" At all events we do not care to multiply points of difference with the United States.

" Canada need have no fear of political affiliation with the British West Indies."

From the foregoing it is plain that the Dominion does not want to become mixed up with our troubles, nor does she seek to help us out of the *bog* ; all that she desires is a chance to dump as much of her product on us as she possibly can, in excess of her purchase of the tropical necessities we send her ; and to receive the cash in return.

While we are not a manufacturing people, yet we have something to sell, which is in the main subject to rapid deterioration, and which, by its frail nature for the most part, requires a near market; failing this, our position would be most precarious.

From this point of view, we find the necessary

conditions readily in the markets of the United States, of which we have been availing ourselves.

For the West Indies, at this moment, to enter into a *most-favoured nation* clause with Canada, whose present ability is to send, but unable to take, would be folly in the extreme.

Not even Britain could ask this of the Dominion : nevertheless, this is in substance what she is endeavouring to extract out of the West Indies, and in which, judging from the trend of the Royal Commission, she apparently has the backing of the Colonial Office at Downing Street.

I presume to say that this is a case of self-preservation for the West Indies, as Canada's position is a decidedly selfish one, since she desires to do to us the very thing she refused to have done to herself.

I offer in substantiation that no sooner had Canada become a self-governing colony than she began to set up tariff barriers against the mother country, who showed a decided inclination to protect herself : yet we find her to-day asking preference of us, knowing full well that such a course would be detrimental to the future welfare of these colonies.

The British West Indies desire to protect themselves to the extent that they do not become a dumping ground, pure and simple, for the Canadian manufactories. We are looking for *reciprocity*.

When Great Britain agreed that the *most-*

favoured nation clause between herself and Germany should be extended to the Dominion, the latter set up such a dismal howl that the concession had to be abrogated in that respect ; and why ? Because she feared the very *outcome* which she is now trying to force upon us—that of becoming the debtor nation.

In the course of the sitting of the Royal Commission in Canada, Mr. T. H. Anson, a representative of the Ogilvie Flour Mills Co., has placed himself on record to this effect :—" If preference were granted by the West Indies, his company would enlarge their plant and go into the business of producing the class of flour most saleable in the tropics."

Such a declaration, on its face, is certainly without one thought for the welfare of the West Indies, but everything for the Canadian merchants, when it is taken into consideration that of over two million barrels of flour exported to the West Indies annually, Canada sends but 9 per cent. of that amount : on what grounds therefore does she ask for preferential treatment ? Is she asking help of us because she finds herself beaten in the race ?

Under such conditions it is manifestly unfair, and a policy of *Self*, pure and simple, that one British possession should attempt such imposition on weaker possessions under the same flag, by insisting on special rates, to which it is not entitled.

As every one knows, and as these figures will

show, we get the bulk of our flour and other supplies from the United States, and she has never yet had to ask any special favours of us. If others are left in the rear through lack of business, tact, or difficulties attendant on natural conditions, we cannot be expected to shoulder the extra burden out of love for the flag.

Even if these colonies were to run the grave risk (which they certainly ought not to do) of extending preference to the Dominion, the latter would find herself handicapped in the matter of transportation facilities, and this handicap she would not be able to overcome for the next twenty years, unless she relied on chartered bottoms to do the service, with the aid of a subsidy from the West Indies, which is not much in evidence at this time. We certainly have had enough of subsidies.

This matter of transportation is but one of the many disadvantages that would confront her should she attempt to corral the West Indian trade in her present unprepared state. We on the other side would be the greater sufferers as a result, to say nothing of the jealousy such an attempt would arouse in the United States, precipitating into a probable crisis.

Canada can well afford to give preference to France over American goods, if she so desires, because she is not by any means dependent on her big neighbour for a market, nor can the United States starve her out at will ; in this her position is quite different from ours. Between the two countries matters seem to be almost equally divided, with the balance of weight on the side of the Dominion.

This is amply shown in a little tariff quarrel since its revision in the United States. The Yankees seem to be so hard hit with their own weapon that they are now of their own accord yelping and calling out for *free trade* with Canada.

The gist of the situation is as follows :—If the United States set up tariff barriers against the Dominion she would be the greater loser before such a war is fairly begun. America wants no tariff war with her northern neighbour if she can avoid it with dignity.

In the year 1908 the United States took from the Dominion the amount of 300,000,000 dollars in raw materials, including *wood pulp*, which is an item of great significance, since the American forests are becoming scanty and will soon be unable to supply the necessary *pulp* which is the life of the newspapers.

Few people are aware of the fact that most of the nickel which goes to harden the armour plate for the American battle-ships comes from Canada : therefore, for these and other reasons, the two countries desire to live in harmony for their mutual benefit.

The Dominion can produce almost every article which she needs for home consumption, excepting such as she must get from the tropics, which is more in the category of luxuries than necessities.

She is therefore infinitely better placed to show favours than the West Indies, in their present crippled condition, and we welcome any and all acts of charity coming from her as a great self-governing colony, rivalled only by her great neighbour the United States ; but to expect any such thing of us seems out of all reason.

For us to declare preferential treatment in favour of Canada, on goods which we now get from the United States, would undoubtedly prove to be an experiment which would bring about certain ruin to the West Indies; more so in the case of Jamaica, which is almost entirely dependent on her markets.

Those who have been watching the course of the recent Tariff Reforms in the United States should bear in mind that there is a clause in the Payne-Aldrick bill, which provides against undue discrimination by foreign countries against the United States, and which compels the administration, in all cases, to impose the *maximum tariff* —25 per cent. *ad valorem*—on all articles from such countries, coming into the United States.

We certainly, knowing the facts of the case and the penalty that would be imposed, should not be in the least eager to create such an uncomfortable situation.

Not only is the United States in a position to retaliate, by imposing the *maximum tariff* on our exports going into that country, but she can also use her influence to divert capital from the States intended for investment in the West Indies (Br.), and to paralyse those already invested.

The British West Indies have no desire to help

the Canadian manufacturers on the *coûte que coûte* plan ; it is purely a matter of business between them, which should be met and dealt with without feeling. We must certainly expect to get a fair return for what we give.

We must be in a position to abandon the American markets, altogether if necessary, before we can talk preference to Canada ; and she, in turn, must be in a position to take all or the greater part of what we produce before we contemplate any step that might be construed by the United States into an affront to her.

CHAPTER XIV

WHEREIN THE DANGER LIES

THE agitation for the annexation of the British West Indian possessions to the United States, which springs up spasmodically at varying periods, would not be considered a very serious matter if the feeling were confined to a few weaklings : but as the scheme has substantial backing, both in the West Indies and in America, we are made to realize that there is more reality in the movement than some are willing to admit.

The acquisition of these tropical possessions of Great Britain, by the *hook* or the *crook*, has been the dream of the people of the United States and the Washington Government for a score or more of years.

It is plain that with Puerto Rico and Panama in her hands, enjoying suzerainty over Cuba and San Domingo, it will only be a question of time before she will be in absolute control of, the entire West Indian group, if something is not done to check this almost irresistible march of conquest.

When allusions with respect to the control of the entire West Indies is made in public places in the United States, the speaker is always greeted with tremendous cheers, which goes to prove the popularity of the suggestion.

That we are not as yet under the American flag, whether we like it or not, is not due to our opposition to the people of that country or to the esteem in which we are held by the mother country : it is simply a matter of time.

The British possessions in the Western Hemisphere have not shown under the Crown Colony system of government such marked progress as to be worthy of special mention. The reason probably lies in the fact that the native population, finding themselves completely overridden by the nominated system, which is enforced in these colonies, have positively lost all interest in the management of the affairs of these possessions.

This system, in some instances, has more to do with the antiquated conditions found in the West Indies than any other circumstance.

It has been pointed out that the harbour improvement of a certain British West Indian Island has been hampered and kept back for many years, necessitating ships destined for that port to anchor far off shore ; and this because the *lighters*, which carry the produce and merchandise to and fro, thus bringing a fair income to their owners, are all tied up with the interest of the nominated and official members of legislature of that colony.

Hence it is to their interest to block legislation to that effect as long as possible, and this they have not failed to do. Why is such a state of affairs permissible under the British flag ?

Because it is no longer possible to run the West Indies from the Colonial Office at Downing Street, with a handful of men in the colonies, and the West Indian committee as advisers, who have their own *axes* to grind.

Such a thing might have been possible half a century ago and probably worked well for that age, but in these days when gain is paramount to honour and justice, the Colonial Office finds its task insurmountable.

There are some who are willing to declare that *juggling with legislation* for personal ends is an impossible thing in a British colony ; but anything is possible in a community where a chosen few are given, and have, the upper hand of all the people, as if these were so many " kaffirs."

In this universal awakening of mankind we hope to be able to rise to the occasion as one man, and by *passive* means endeavour to stem the tide of retrogression, and to reclaim the West Indies from the depths into which they have fallen, with the hope of nursing them back to their former selves, and thus preserve the West Indies for the West Indians and their posterity.

I counsel *passiveness*, for to do anything worth doing, with any degree of success, patience and self-restraint, *not violence* and *indiscretion*, are the necessary ingredients of success.

Inflammatory speakers, appealing to ignorance and to all such acts as have in them a tendency to stir up strife, would produce but one effect on the minds of the British public (who, say what you please, have the last word as to whether we shall have responsible government or not), which would be that we are not as yet fit to take to ourselves the reins of self-government.

By a single rash or untimely act the labours of a quarter of a century may be swept away and leave us naked, without a hope, for another generation : we must therefore proceed with much care, tact, and forbearance, if our efforts for better conditions are to be crowned with success.

Sedition, seditious language, unpatriotic and revolutionary utterances do more harm to our present position, to the cause of self-government for which we are now arming ourselves, than some of our supposed leaders imagine.

Already there is a section of the population of one of our most important colonies, that is accusing the native press of that island of declaring for annexation to the United States, and, notwithstanding that such accusations are without the slightest foundation, it goes to show the temper of the people towards any such move, but which cannot, I fear, forestall the *inevitable*.

If we take the late action of Admiral Davis of the United States Navy (although coupled with humanitarian principles) when he peremptorily set aside the duly authorized executive authority during the catastrophe at Kingston, Jamaica (an *authority* which Englishmen of no less renown than the late Sir Alfred Jones held sacred even at such a crisis and refused to interfere), landed his marines under arms, erected tents upon British soil over which flew the Stars and Stripes alone : if we take this as an instance of American domination of the West Indies, then it is clear what their purpose is, without exception, as regards the future of these possessions.

Jamaica and her sister colonies owe much to ex-Governor Swettenham for the stand he took on that occasion, when all others seem to have lost their bearings in preserving the dignity of the British nation and flag, and in postponing this moral Yankee invasion, the forerunner of annexation.

In spite of the misleading cables which were caused to be sent out from American and other sources, branding the natives of that island as the most despicable souls, Sir Alexander Swettenham demonstrated to the world that there was no such grave peril, as seen through American eyes, to be feared from the negroes of Jamaica.

He rightly dismissed the American armed force, in maintenance of his conviction that military display other than that which the island afforded was an unnecessary and dangerous element, and that the situation could take care of itself because the people were law-abiding and mindful of the rights of others, even in times of sore affliction and great peril.

Subsequent events proved that he was correct in his judgment of the conduct to be expected of the people of Kingston, Jamaica.

In the *Cruise of the Port Kingston*, already referred to, a book written by Hall Caine, a novelist of world-wide fame, who, by the way, is an Englishman, it is given out to the world that considerable " looting was carried on by the natives (negroes) and that oftentimes the looter was looted by the soldiery."

It is to be hoped that the accusation was only based on rumours of a slanderous nature against men whose coolness and personal bravery on this very occasion deserve commendation instead of condemnation.

No one doubts that looting to some insignificant and trivial extent was carried on ; but in what country is looting conspicuously absent on such trying occasions ?

Looting was done in London to an alarming proportion in the fire that occurred during the ravages of the black-death in 1356. It occurred during the fires at Moscow in 1812 ; Hamburg in 1842 ; Paris in 1871 ; Chicago in the same year, and in Boston in 1872. It was done more recently in San Francisco during the disaster caused by earthquake ; and at Messina, Italy, where it was necessary to bring firearms into play.

Crime is but crime, whether committed by black or white : therefore it seems out of the question to expect the world to go into hysterics because black men have taken to looting and robbing the dead—a field which, from superstitious fear of the dead among the negroes, had been heretofore exclusively monopolized by white men.

Looting has no particular affinity to any race of people, and so long as these disasters continue, this crime of crimes will always be committed the world over ; and no law or government will be able totally to prevent it.

The bitterness with which the author of the *Cruise of the Port Kingston* assailed the negro populace and soldiery of Kingston, Jamaica, tends to demonstrate his animosity towards the negro race. This feeling is more conspicuous throughout his book than the truth of his statement that all Kingston went mad because they saw something to steal.

That reminds one of the *iron safe* episode which was gallantly rescued by *white sailors* from a gang of *negro looters*, but which failed to turn up when the Governor asked that it be produced.

Returning to the subject, we ask ourselves, why do we fear annexation when almost every man, woman, and child, with a drop of negro blood (and they comprise nine-tenths of the population) is in opposition to the scheme ?

For answer, I point to the Panama Canal, now nearing completion ; the abrogation of the Clayton-Bulwer Treaty by which Great Britain " renounces her right to construct and control " the Nicaragua Canal ; the strong and ever-increasing friendship between these two great English-speaking nations ; the constant desire of the older nation to meet the younger one *more than* halfway in all matters of controversy. All these I submit, go to endanger the life of the

British West Indian possessions as British territory.

There is also another reason, which, although purely local, contains some element of apprehension.

Some fifteen years ago or more, a body of farmers, West Indians, now naturalized citizens of the United States, sent a letter to the State Department in which they asked that the Government of the United States take steps to annex the Island of Jamaica—a British West Indian possession.

Such a letter ought to be in existence to-day, and I am informed by one of the men concerned, that the reply was, in substance, that any such request must come from the Island Legislature, which appeared to have been the only requisite lacking to demand official notice.

How many such appeals may have been made from similar and other sources I am unable to say. It is enough that the one alluded to was made beyond the question of a doubt.

The chief danger, however, lies in the strategical position which Jamaica will bear to the Panama Canal when this waterway shall have been completed, and which in all essentials will be a military waterway.

Jamaica to the United States corresponds exactly with the position which Heligoland— formerly a British possession at the mouth of the River Elbe, in the North Sea—bore to Germany's interest and which prompted its acquisition by the latter government from Great Britain for a German concession in Central Africa.

Judging from the similarity in the situation, there are some who are willing to stake their all that such will be the destiny of Jamaica if she is not bought outright, and that America will be the Germany in this case.

The inhabitants of the Lesser Antilles look at the matter of the annexation of the Island of Jamaica to the United States as a subject of total indifference to them.

" If it does happen it will not affect us," some have been heard to say, but they overlook the fact that *Jamaica* is one of our most important colonies, and that it would be as *bad an omen* to allow her to pass from British control, if united action can prevent it, as the omission of the words *our Dominion beyond the Seas*, in King George the Fifth's proclamation to the United Empire, upon his accession to the throne.

The *Press* of these colonies treat the matter from a parochial point of view, in a semi-sympathetic manner by way of comment, but not in the way to suggest that it is of vital importance to their very existence as British Colonies. Quite possibly it matters little to them who will be their next owner. My only hope is that it will not end like the case of *Tom* in *Uncle Tom's Cabin*.

Now, as a matter of fact, just as the taking over of Jamaica by the United States might be necessary for the better protection of the Panama

Canal, so Trinidad, Barbados, and British Guiana for that matter, might be an absolute necessity to that same power, in the carrying out of her policing policy, and in the exercise of the *Monroe Doctrine* in neighbouring South American Republics.

Who will say her *no* ! if she elects to have them at all cost ? Not England, I am sure.

Her policy in these days is not shaped on the plans which were carried out by *Rodney* and *Nelson* : it is now everything for peace, at least with America.

If these Latin Republics were to combine and declare war against the United States, spurred on by Japan or Germany, in an effort to check Yankee aggression, that country would find it extremely hard to carry on a successful war with these countries without a base or coaling station in close proximity with all its other advantages, when other nations declare their neutrality.

If she is to take upon her broad shoulders the task of keeping these warring South American nations in order, and as it is quite likely, judging from passing events, that they will not thus tamely submit to any outside interference with the programme in this respect, the prognosis is that trouble of a grave nature will surely ensue, and in order to demonstrate her predominant position before the world, warlike preparations will promptly supersede persuasive measures, only to find that she is without a foothold in these parts.

Surely this is a truly vexed question to confront a great, ambitious, and dignified nation like America ; and as some avenue must be found out of this most embarrassing position, it naturally casts a gloom over the entire West Indian Group, which offers the only solution, and whose status is consequently endangered.

To-day we find the Americans, for some deep-seated reason, taking exception to the coming into being of a Canadian navy as an adjunct to the Imperial Defence Scheme, and it is almost certain that they would show strong disapproval at this juncture, if England should suddenly begin formidable fortifications in the West Indies —which, should war come between the two nations, would place the United States on a defensive footing.

Although a clash of arms between the two nations, unless drawn on by outside interest, is hardly possible, yet the Americans are not taking any chances by which their supremacy in the Atlantic Ocean and Caribbean Sea might be threatened—they are leaving no stone unturned.

The question uppermost in the minds of every serious and liberty-loving West Indian, at this moment is : Will America in course of time, emboldened by Britain's pacific demeanour towards her, ask the latter to turn over her West Indian possessions to the United States, and remove her flag from these waters as did France in the case of Louisiana ?

In such an event would England, out of feeling

for an alien race that she had nursed and cared for—some of them for more than two centuries—be willing to risk the displeasure of the United States rather than pass us off for a consideration, and abandon us to whatever fate might await us ? *Quien sabe ?*

The reply to such a demand would depend greatly on the relative position of the two nations at such a time, which at present is not hard to forecast for the next twenty years, the balance of power being in favour of America.

As the sale of the West Indies, before the finding of oil in Trinidad and copper in Jamaica in paying quantities, has been advocated more than once by parties in England and America, it is safe to say that such a forecast is not entirely out of the realm of ordinary politics.

In spite of these gloomy forebodings, choosing between the two fires, it can be said without fear of contradiction that we wish to remain British in spite of our internal disagreement ; we wish to remain as much as possible independent of the United States : we wish to be *federated* as one body with *self-government*, and to be given an opportunity to build up the West Indies back to their former selves.

We have progressive ideas and plans ; we wish for an opportunity to develop, as civilized men, what can be well termed *one national business* in our own way, with the kind assistance of the mother country.

Confederation of the British West Indian

Colonies with *responsible government* is the only condition that will save us from the " coming events " which have manifestly cast their shadows before.

As confederated colonies under self-government, we should be more British than ever, and should be in a superior position to make terms with Canada and the United States on a basis satisfactory to all parties concerned, and thus insure a market, under liberal terms, for a stated number of years.

If we must remain another ten years under Crown Colony system of government, we are the liable to be left out in the cold when the United States, our largest customer, decides that the time has arrived when her markets can be supplied with tropical products from her own colonies.

Great Britain, in appointing a commission to consider the best means of fostering trade relations between Canada and the West Indies, foresaw the approaching climax, and, being mindful of our future prosperity, is doing her utmost to save the situation.

The effort is well made and with all good intent, but there are many who are of the opinion that she has allowed the *disease* to progress too far, and consequently the *remedies* which are now being applied will be of little or no avail.

Canada is a young, powerful, and growing country, possessing enormous possibilities, endeavouring to establish herself in the commercial world, the success of which depends on her ability to build up a great world trade in the face of the very keen competition of the present day ; to rear up a merchant marine ; to develop freely her business connections and to embrace every possible opportunity, as it presents itself ; to gain a part of the West Indian trade which, although over a century old, is still in its infancy.

All this, however, necessarily means time, and time, being her own mistress, can neither be hurried nor delayed. In the meantime our condition becomes more and more deplorable, for " while the grass grows the horse starves."

Allowing for all the glowing promises which Canada has in store for the future, to lure the West Indian trade to her markets, it is certain that, were it possible to take a census of the opinion of the people of the West Indies on the matter of their preference and trade between Canada and the United States, it would be found that nine-tenths of the people would be unanimously in favour of the continuance of the present trade relations with America.

Distance, rigid winters, small population, poor transportation and communication, obstacles which cannot be overcome in a day, are a few of the many disadvantages against the Canadian markets.

Apart from the points already enumerated as contributing against the markets of the Dominion, and in favour of those of the United States as far as the West Indies are concerned, the American manufacturers appear to possess superior ability and facility to cater for the needs of the people of the tropics in which the Canadian and English seem to be woefully lacking.

Great Britain is correct in her fears that we shall ultimately be practically ousted from the American markets, and were it not for the fact of the realization of the approaching calamity, there probably would never have been appointed a *Royal Commission* on Trade between the West Indies and the Dominion.

We, too, fear this end unless a change is made in the present system of government in these His Majesty's West Indian possessions, giving us a free hand to look out for, and protect more fully, our own interest.

One can hardly conceive how the British people—a liberty-loving nation—can thus close their eyes and conscience to the fact that we, as civilized human beings, are entitled to the same scope of liberty which Englishmen enjoy at home.

As matters stand we are no better off than so many slaves, in spite of our loyalty to the Crown and all that we may profess otherwise.

We look to our present sovereign, King George V., that he will use his great influence with the leaders of the Government to treat us with that just consideration which we deserve, by granting us the privilege of *responsible government* which has been so freely granted to Australia, Canada, and South Africa.

This attempt to awaken the British people and Government to their strict sense of justice towards the West Indies and West Indians must not be looked upon as the appeal of a single individual ; indeed not. It is the cry of millions to be relieved from bondage and excessive toil as is their right as living beings ; and which has been echoed and re-echoed through the press of these colonies in one form or the other, and now finally in book form.

The *Jamaica Gleaner* under date May 26, 1910, under the heading, "A Policy for Jamaica," asked many pertinent questions. It says :

" Have we, or have we not, arrived at the parting of the ways ? Are we to continue satisfied with the presence of a Government numerical majority in the Legislative Council, or shall we seek for the restoration of the former elected majority ? Is the country fit to have an elected majority in the Legislative Council ? Has the Legislative Council proved itself capable of exercising intelligently the political power and privileges with which it is endowed ? Are the men in the country willing and able to represent the electors in the Legislative Council of Jamaica ?

" All these questions, it seems to us, should be asked to-day, for the time has arrived for asking them. We stand on the threshold of a new decade. Are we to continue marking time, or are we to go forward ? We believe that the time has come when we should go forward.

" Now let us see briefly how, during the last ten years the elected element of the Legislative Council has acted. It has kept a check upon Government expenditure. It has assisted in an endeavour to place the finance of this island in a strong condition, and to provide to some extent against future contingencies.

" It has shown great readiness and willingness to work with the Government whenever the Government has been right.   In spite of considerable abuse, it has shown a remarkable devotion to duty ; and, in spite of all sneers to the contrary, it has displayed ability in dealing with public questions.   Moderation has been the keynote of its career.

" It has shown that opposition to any particular government proposal is not opposition to the government, or to the British authority in this Island.   In view of all these facts and circumstances, *is it necessary or wise, or just*, that the elected members should continue to occupy a position of numerical inferiority in the House ? We think not, and in a subsequent article we shall give further reasons which we hope will appeal to every man of intelligence who takes interest in Jamaica."

This is only the cry of one colony, but it echoes the prevailing sentiment in the breast of every man and woman of the sister colonies, and there will be no rest, no let up, until relief comes : the relief by *responsible government*, which we are in every sense fitted to take up and carry out successfully.   We have no desire that the change should come upon us overnight—we want it to come step by step until the whole change is effected.

Responsible government for the West Indies cannot be condemned before it is tried, and even if it fails at the first trial that would be no foundation on which to base the belief that it should not be tried a second time, yea, a third and a fourth time, until it is successfully established.

We have it on record that when this form of government was first tried in Canada it was an absolute failure; but did it not succeed upon a second trial?

PART III

FEDERATION, WITH COLONIAL SELF-GOVERNMENT

CHAPTER XV

THE FEDERATION

THE changes that would follow confederation of the British West Indian possessions under *responsible government* are many, but one of the first benefits that would be derived from such a union would be the off-setting of the possibility of annexation to the United States, rendering all further agitation to this end fruitless, if not altogether impossible ; and to reserve these colonies for the British Crown by removing them beyond the pale of outside political pressure and bringing them under the protection of colonial self-government.

There are some who will ask : How is it that a federation of the West Indies under responsible government would remove them from the political arena and hence the danger of their being annexed to the United States of America ?

In answer it is only necessary to say that there being no likelihood of America going to war with Britain for her (Britain's) possessions in the West Indies, that item being settled as far as common reasoning will permit, there remain only the possibilities of her selling them outright for a

cash consideration, passing them over as compen-
sation for some political support at a crucial
moment, or exchanging them for the Philippines—
this last proposition being the least likely.

If, however, these colonies were federated under
colonial self-government, their destiny would be
entirely in the hands of the inhabitants in certain
respects, and Britain would be debarred from
making away with them under political pressure,
while she would have all the power in preventing
them from entering into any compact that would
in the slightest measure endanger her sovereignty.

Once the measures are granted they would be
zealously guarded by the natives of these possessions who would do all in their power to preserve
them, and would never think of allowing themselves to be again subjugated by another power.
In this way I reason that " we should be removed
from the political arena " and hence from annexation to the United States.

Opinion will naturally differ, as on all other
matters, about the confederation of the West
Indies (British) under self-government, but in
spite of such differences, which cannot but come
from the *enemies of liberty*, the weak-kneed, and
such as possess no personal merit, I firmly believe that ninety-nine per cent. of the people
inhabiting these possessions will coincide with
me, that the benefits to be derived from such a
union are many and important.

All of us, more or less, are willing to concur
that America would not, under present condi-

tions, attempt to gain the British West Indies by resorting to a clash of arms ; such a course the mind refuses to grasp ; but it must be admitted as possible that, as long as they continue under the Crown Colony system of government, they are, in a sense, mere chattels in the hands of the British Government, and consequently are subject to conveyance.

Our position, therefore, is an extremely perilous one, as anything is likely to happen at any moment, to embarrass the Home Government greatly, which may materially change conditions with regard to England's sovereignty over these possessions.

It is *perilous*, because, should the question of their transfer come up for consideration, and Britain refuse to hand them over to the United States for policy, love, or money, the latter will at once attribute such a refusal to ulterior motives, which would possibly bring about a misunderstanding, much to be deplored, between these two great English-speaking nations.

In such a case she would only have to bide her time until an opportunity offered itself, at a moment when England was engaged in a war and had her hands full; then she would pounce down upon us.

Confederation, with self-government, would be a protection in peace or war—under such conditions we would fear no foe.

It is the opinion of some of the clearest observers, that the continuance of the West Indian possessions of Great Britain under the *present form of government* will contribute to results which will in the near future threaten seriously her supremacy over them, if not on the seas.

If war comes with Germany, as every one expects, unless the conflict is waged exclusively in European waters, which is hardly probable on the part of Germany, thirsting as she is after expansion and a great German Empire, England will find herself absolutely incapable of giving ample protection to her numerous colonies.

The particular connection of such a grave situation with regard to her West Indian possessions is that she might find it to her interest to pass us temporarily under the American flag, for the matter of safe keeping, if when such a war comes it unfortunately finds us still staggering under the weight of Crown Colony government, without any means of protecting our homes and country.

In such an event, it is expected that the *most important* colonies (colonies with exclusively white population) who are weak in their defences would receive such assistance as could be spared from England, but the West Indies with negro populations would be left to shuffle out the best way they could.

The self-governing colonies are now preparing for such an emergency by their naval and military preparations; but the West Indies under Crown Colony government, dissected from each other, each pulling against the other, headed by cliques of men who have for generations been running the government their own way for personal ends ; men who look upon *any reform* that upsets their calculations as attacking their *hereditary* ownership of certain government offices ; is plodding along in the same old way, fully cognizant of the danger ahead, but unmindful of it or its consequences.

We are without adequate military protection against an invading foe, no matter how puny, and also without any form of naval support : nor can we expect any.

Could we not have made similar efforts to provide these, in the manner of Canada or Australia, if we were federated and granted colonial self-government ?

Most assuredly ! But as long as things are managed from Downing Street, which is thousands of miles away from the base of operations, so long shall we remain with our hands tied, impotent to do anything, notwithstanding that the mind is active, and the body alert and willing to do.

If England were victorious over the Germans all would be well with us, and at the close of the war we might find ourselves under the *old banner* ; but if the unexpected happened, and there were another Tugela, a Colenso, Spion Kop, or Magersfontein, which some of those skilled in military tactics say is not at all unlikely, and England were defeated on sea and land, it would be a matter of option to the United States whether she should keep or return us to the *old control* which, defeated and crippled, would be unable to enforce her demands.

We should be entirely at the mercy of the Yankees, who, with a great modern navy and the most intelligent body of volunteers the world has ever known, eager and ready to flock to her standard, would readily and unblushingly assume the rôle of dictator to the world.

This is plainly seen in the high hand which the United States has played in the politics of Europe, South America, and in the Far East. From a West Indian point of view, therefore, the defeat of Great Britain would be a great calamity to civilization.

With all the peacemaking proclivities of our late sovereign, King Edward VII., and unpleasant as it is for a British subject to admit, England is indeed not the beloved nation of Europe; she should therefore be in a position to watch her friends as well as her enemies, and to take the defensive or the offensive should the occasion demand the necessity.

On the other hand, after a long-drawn-out contest, win or lose, money may be of the first importance to the British Government, and in such an emergency the attention of the English people would be first directed to their West Indian possessions, for which they would find a ready purchaser in the Government of the United States.

When men stand under the very shadow of being sold in bulk, with their families, houses and lands, should they not seek to avert such a pending calamity ? Certainly ! The only safeguard, however, lies in confederation, with colonial self-government.

The alarmists, who are the opponents of *responsible government* for the West Indies, will be heard with their usual dismal howl about the riots, rebellion, and other petty strifes which, they will say, are sure to follow ; but all such anticipated outbursts are mere ghost stories, without any foundation, and can have little or no effect on the situation.

There are others who are ready to come forward with the declaration that if we were granted colonial self-government we shall ultimately strike out boldly for absolute independence, and thus cause the mother country some anxiety.

To this class I desire to point out that Canada and Australia, who have had experience along those lines, desire no greater scope than that which they now enjoy ; for not only are they protected and helped in developing their natural resources by Great Britain, but they are being made allies of the world's greatest power on land and sea.

Surely that is something to which to cling and be justly proud of ; and the hope of the United West Indies is to be initiated into this most exclusive circle before another score of years are passed. These self-governing colonies are therefore better secured than if they actually had their own independence, and the same feeling of security would be experienced by the West Indian colonies under federation, with responsible government : there would and could be no thought of separation from the mother country.

But for this great protecting force, Australia would readily become the prey of ambitious Japan ; the United States would dominate Canada ; and Germany would most willingly do the honours for United South Africa.

Under the present arrangements, however, these colonies can afford to go to bed with the feeling that, as long as England is supreme on the ocean, no other nation dare attack them before daybreak, or at any other time for that matter, without having to reckon with the united British Empire.

Remove this overpowering force, and the whole combination is shattered to atoms.

The drift of the situation can therefore be summed up as follows :—The colonies have no desire to part from the parental care of the mother country : what they most desire is to be able to be of some assistance to her, if need be, and to be permitted to manage their own affairs as civilized, intelligent, and liberty-loving people.

CHAPTER XVI

THE RETRENCHMENT

THE confederation of the West Indies being primarily an economical consideration, among the first items to be considered, therefore, would be *retrenchment* in the running of the Union Government.

Under such consideration one can venture to say that the subject of the salaries of our colonial officials would claim the highest attention.

There are some questions, however, which must be satisfactorily answered, if the matter of the reduction of our colonial officials is to be dealt with in an impartial manner ; they are as follows :

First. Are the governors and other public officers of the various British West Indian possessions too highly paid for their services ?

Second. Having regard for size of country, class of inhabitants, and financial condition, is there a comparison where the officials receive similar salaries ?

Third. Could we, under confederation, dispense with the services of these over-abundantly paid men for less expensive ones, without detriment to the union ?

Fourth. Can the West Indian colonies afford to pay out such large sums in salaries without increasing the already great burden of the poor taxpayers ?

If these questions can be answered satisfactorily in the *affirmative*, then we have no cause for complaint ; but the replies must be returned in the negative, and therefore the situation would call for immediate remedy by the opponents of the fleecers of the Government.

Let us take Jamaica and Trinidad as examples.

These islands, which are together but a speck of land when compared with Canada or Australia, are both called upon to contribute the exorbitant sum of £5,000 annually to a governor, besides furnishing him with residence, assistants, travelling expenses and other accompanying luxuries, which figure up to more than an extra £2,000, making a grand total of over seven thousand pounds (£7,000) per annum.

It is to be hoped that no body of independent legislators who have their country's interest at heart would contemplate the voting of a sum of seven thousand pounds sterling as a salary for the Governor-General of the United West Indies.

With a governor-general at headquarters, wherever this may be, it would only be necessary to have lieutenant-governors or administrators in the other colonies to assist him in carrying out the wishes of the legislators.

Such sub-governors would be considered well paid if they received a salary of £1,800 per annum for Jamaica and Trinidad (a sum £200 less than the salary of the governor of the State of New York); the amount paid by the other possessions being compatible with their financial status.

We cannot but admit that we are carrying things high, living as millionaires when we are in reality *paupers*. This fact is forcibly brought out when we recollect that the Island of Jamaica pays her chief justice £2,000 per annum, which is only £100 less than the salary of a chief justice of the United States.

As a result of the excessive drainage on the population's finances, the condition of the peasantry of both countries bears no comparison whatever.

In the United States the bulk of the population are well clothed, well fed, and well housed, while all that His Majesty's subjects in the West Indies can boast of is that they are, for the most part, an *impoverished, beggarly-looking, barefooted* lot of peasants, of whose unfortunate condition any civilized and progressive government ought to be ashamed.

Can we as an intelligent people take pride in seeing our women and children compelled, from sheer necessity, to coal ships; to tramp miles with heavy loads on their heads ; and to go barefooted, in order to provide means with which to pay their ever-increasing taxation, while those who reap the *blood-money* in large salaries sleep on beds of roses, and at the end retire with a pension for the rest of their days ? Never ! It is human to complain, but surely there is ample justification for our present dissatisfaction.

How much longer will this cruel, crushing, and overbearing state of affairs be permitted to continue, in the face of all that is right and just before God and man, is the question which is of concern to every serious-minded West Indian.

Of the forty-nine states and territories comprising the United States of America, only three of the most important ones—namely, New York, New Jersey, and Pennsylvania—pay their governors £2,000 per year : three thousand pounds less than Jamaica or Trinidad.

The remuneration for the chief executive of the remaining states and territories ranges from between five hundred and a thousand pounds.

Now, as a matter of fact, the State of West Virginia, which has a population slightly in excess of the Island of Jamaica, pays its governor the modest sum of £600 per annum.

When we compare statistics, however, we find that West Virginia abounds in coal mines, has *ten million* acres under farming, produces *sixty million* gallons of milk, *fourteen million* pounds of butter, *seventy-four* thousand pounds of cheese, *two and a half million* pounds of wool, *five million* pounds of tobacco annually, as compared with the very trivial resources of Jamaica, Trinidad, Barbados, British Guiana, and Honduras, and the rest of the other West Indian islands put together.

At the time of writing, capitalists all over

England are going mad about the Trinidad *oil fields*, and the glorious prospects which are before them as investors ; on the other hand, the peasantry of the island are asking each other whether the *Home Office* will not become affected by the craze, and thus add another thousand or more pounds to the chief executive's salary, or make it two governors instead of one.

While such a step would not be looked upon as possible, and is hardly feasible, yet, as everything with regard to the West Indies is done without thought for the wishes of the majority of the inhabitants, one may expect *anything* to happen at any time.

Confederation would centralize the administration, lessen the expense of running the government, and, as a result, bring relief to the overburdened taxpayers : but confederation and centralization without *responsible government* would work more harm than good, and place additional obstacles in our path, rather than prosperity. The one without the other as a necessary part would be tantamount to placing a double-edged sword in the hands of the colonial office and the " West Indian Committee."

Five thousand pounds annually for a governor's salary is exactly half the amount paid to the Governor-Generals of Canada, Australia, and South Africa, any of which taken separately is many hundred times more prosperous than the combined prosperity of all the West Indies.

It is evident that salaries paid to the Governor-

Generals of these great self-governing colonies are not taken as a standard on which to base those of the governors of the West Indies. If it were so, surely our burden would be infinitely less.

The average West Indian cannot be made to believe that his colony is half as prosperous as Canada, Australia, or South Africa; consequently he fails to comprehend why his governor-general should be paid half as much as the governor-general of one of these great self-governing colonies.

Many persons believe that if the bulk of the population of the West Indies were whites instead of a servile lot of blacks and mixed-breds, the Home Government would think more than twice before imposing such a heavy and unjustifiable task upon them; for no white race would so easily submit to taxation without representation.

It would indeed be a sad case if I were the only one who is of the opinion that our officials are too highly paid, and that the Government would be better off with less of these important personages: indeed, fair-minded Englishmen and thousands of others in America and the West Indies are also of this opinion.

Did not the late Thomas Summerbell, M.P. (Sunderland), on January 28, 1908, call the attention of the Home Government in the House of Commons to the existing state of affairs in the West Indies?

He asserted that

" the administration in His Majesty's West Indian Colonies were altogether too costly, and that it imposed on the people of these islands an enormous burden of taxation, which was altogether out of proportion to what it should be.

Continuing, he said :

" The revenue of the islands two years ago amounted to £3,000,000 sterling, and how was that raised ?

" The governors of these islands were considerably overpaid, as compared with governors of self-governing colonies.

" In Tasmania, with an average export of £16 per head, the governor's salary was £2,500 annually.

" In Jamaica, where the export was £2 per head, the governor's salary was £5,000 per annum.

It might be interesting to note that Tasmania fell into the hands of the English in 1803 and in 1856—fifty-three years after, it was given responsible government.

" We ought to commence," continued the honourable gentleman, " by reducing the salaries of these governors.

" The importation of coolies to these places from India had reduced the wages to thirty-four cents per day, and they objected to the subsidy of £8,000 which was taken out of the revenue derived from taxation to bring in this cheap labour."

These are but few of our ills that have found ventilation in the House of Commons, but behind the scenes there are many tales to tell : dead men's bones ! dead men's bones ! ! on every side, some of which may never see the light of day.

In these His Majesty's Colonies, unlike England, where the law is so elastic that it can be stretched to make almost every unpopular expression of the mind a misdemeanour, no one dares to tell the true nature of these *tales behind the scenes*, whether they be graft or mismanagement.   My readers are therefore left to draw their own conclusion from the following article taken from the Port of Spain *Mirror*, a daily paper (owned by a Scotsman) in the Island of Trinidad, dated April 27, 1910.

" Fresh Taxation " is the title of the editorial, which goes on to say :

" The meeting of the Legislative Council to-day promises to be of considerable importance to the inhabitants of the Colony in general, and the proceedings should be noted with attention. We understand that one of the principal items to be discussed will be fresh taxation to the extent of £50,000 for five years, and the ostensible reason for levying this *extra burden* is the need of better roads, with proper iron bridges.

" It is said that the roads have been starved for years, and that now we have to put them in order, because of a cheeseparing policy in the past.

" It would be *more honest* (continued the journal) if the Government explained how *thousands* upon *thousands* of *pounds* sterling have been spent upon the *Paria Government* road, along the north coast, and *which* is *only to be found* on the map, and upon other roads which are *almost non-existent.* Another reason is to meet the demands created by motor traffic.

" In view of the recent taxes imposed upon the people in the form of higher customs duties, this new attempt at taxation creates a very disagreeable feeling.

" By these taxes it was proposed to raise £50,000 ; but we are informed that the Government have been able to raise at least £60,000 by them.

" Although the Government only raises this amount, however, the poor consumers, owing to the inability of merchants and shop-keepers to properly apportion the new increase, have to pay an increased price for almost every single article of consumption, and consequently, instead of the figure being £60,000 it would more likely amount to £120,000.

" This any fair-minded person would regard as a sufficiently heavy burden on the majority of the inhabitants, but the Government, although quite aware of this fact, still proposes to raise another £50,000, so that they may be able with the surplus, estimated now at £30,000, to carry on the extraordinary work by spending £80,000, for five years.

" We are all aware that taxes originally stated to be temporarily imposed have always been made permanent locally, and the consequent outlook does not seem to be very encouraging.

" We have been further informed that the taxes will be raised among other items, by doubling the land tax, creating a wheel tax, and imposing taxes on aerated waters, etc. Our impression was that the £50,000 recently raised was for public works extraordinary, and we never entertained the idea that additional sums would be required.

"Surely if it were found necessary to raise more money temporarily, recourse could be had to loans, the interest on which could easily be met by the surplus obtained under the new tariff.

"If the increase of motor traffic necessitates extra burden, we think that motors should be made to contribute the greater part of the sum.

"The doubling of the land tax will tell heavily on the poor peasant proprietors, who already have to pay dearer for their food and clothing, while in the meantime the price of their produce has fallen.

"These people, as a matter of fact, already experience difficulty in meeting their annual taxes, and the result of these taxes will be to deprive them of these little plots of ground and their homes.

"We have also heard it proposed to raise a tax on land in connection with the road-boards. How will the poor people meet all this ? *It is time that some united and determined effort* should be made to prevent this *continual imposition* of burdens, without giving the people a voice in managing their affairs.

"The public should make some protest against these measures, or they will soon find themselves faced by further exactions. In the *great self-governing dependencies* of the Empire, permanent works are always defrayed by loans extending over a period of years.

"Were it otherwise and these great countries had been compelled to defray the cost out of current revenue, they would never have gone ahead as they have done.

"Apparently the small colonies are not to be allowed to do this. If this is so it is time the taxpayers got a move on, and showed the Government that they must be consulted, and that they must have a very large and a very real and all-powerful voice in the spending of public money."

These are fair examples of mismanagement, if nothing else, under the present system of government in the West Indies, and from which we may learn some valuable lessons on *retrenchment* for the uplifting and ultimate benefit of our down-trodden West Indian community. This is a case where the press of Trinidad is bold enough to speak on the subject, but we all know that Trinidad is not the only colony which is struggling under this unequal load.

Unfortunately we have no method of showing the Government that we must be consulted in all such matters. The Government of the West Indian colonies is that in which the minority rules.

We hope and wait with the expectation that " all good things come to those that wait."

CHAPTER XVII

EDUCATIONAL FACILITIES

WHAT is education ? The subject is defined as :
" That process which draws out the power of
the character of an individual, and not the
putting of information into the mind. Its chief
product is not knowledge, nor success, but power—
power of the mind and body, guided by power
of will."

When one notes the very meagre facilities for
giving our children a free extensive education,
one cannot but ask whether this end can be
attained when our children are asked to leave the
elementary schools at the tender age of fourteen
years, without any means of securing a higher free
education.

Can the great end which education seeks to
attain be accomplished, if we discourage our
elementary schoolmasters by paying them wages
which are not in keeping with their wants, and by
robbing them of the privileges of promotion ?

The college professor is all right in his way, but
he couldn't teach Classics to a boy who does not
understand the rudiments of the lower branches
of education, which is the work of the elementary

teacher, and which counts, of all, as the greater factor in the future career of the boy or girl.

As the bricklayer who lays an inferior foundation for want of interest in his work, or because he is poorly paid. therefor, and his work collapses as soon as the heavier structures are placed thereon, so does the elementary teacher who, for want of proper encouragement and an adequate salary, crams his scholars in order to keep his school up to a money-making standard, to the detriment of the children, many of whom become absolutely unfit to grapple with the higher studies, when these are placed before them.

Such results can be summed up in two words —bad foundation. Bad foundation in anything, whether it be education or bricklaying, endangers the life of the superstructure. To accomplish the results which education aims to bring about, the barriers to a *thorough* system of *free education* must be unreservedly removed, and a scheme which will enable a child to start from the very lowest grade, until he completes his college education at the Government's expense, must be inaugurated and maintained.

Such *free education* shall be without limit or specific time, and not subjected to a special or particular standing or ability to be judged by competitive tests.

Under confederation, with responsible government, the economical and administrative advantages would be so improved by virtue of retrenchment and an independent legislature, that not only would our elementary schoolmasters receive better financial treatment and the humane consideration to which they are entitled, but the schools and children would also receive better attention than they now do, or can ever hope to receive under the present conditions.

Modern education, after allowing for proper housing, benching, and desking (in which particulars our elementary schools are conspicuously deficient), should provide that all schoolrooms be instructively decorated with pictures and paintings which tend to chivalry or patriotism, in keeping with the progress of modern times.

Maps and saintly pictures are not the only requisites of adornment a school should be allowed ; there should also be pictures and illustrations of ancient and modern inventions ; of ancient and modern warfare ; of the latest scientific and astronomical improvements, etc., which tend to build up a great and broad mind in its preparation for the reception of an equally broad education. There can be no question that *compulsory free education* * is for the betterment of every people ; and its influence has been amply felt in those countries in which this system is inaugurated and enforced.

The ancient Persians and Spartans long recognized the necessity of such a course, and paid great attention not only to the moral but also to the *political* and *military* training of their children

* Since the writing of this book Jamaica has declared for compulsory education.

along compulsory lines. It was in 1524 that Luther drew up the scheme of compulsory free education, and which Frederick the Great of Prussia enforced throughout his dominions in 1793. A similar condition had been in force in France previous to that, under Louis XV., almost a century before, when attendance *up to any age* was free to all.

In Scotland there is at present a secondary free education, but this condition is very much exceeded in the United States by a *third* and still a *fourth* stage in all public schools, which accounts for the great and rapid advancement of the American negro and the population in general.

The system permits of a child, after passing through the eight primary grades, to enter the High School, and from thence, after completing a four years' course, he passes on to the college preparatory course, at which he spends two years, and then a final college course of four more years which completes his education, *free of all cost.*

With this preparation he passes on to the world's stage to do *his turn*—certainly better equipped than the heavily burdened West Indian taxpayer's son, who is compelled by law to leave the public school at a very tender age to wander about aimlessly, unfit to exercise the franchise of an intelligent citizen.

This is a necessary condition (*the free-up-to-any-age system*) which is highly suited for the West Indies (British) with their large population of *illiterates* ; but the remedy is not in our hands to cure the disease and it will never be until we shall have been federated and granted responsible government, or its equivalent.

Under a united and economical government, with our own interest in our own hands, there is no reason to believe that we should long delay the scheme of compulsory free education throughout the confederacy.

It is a patent fact, the world over, wherever the influence of the white man predominates, be he English or American, that the feeling is : Educate the negro and you spoil him ; make him a free man and he refuses to work. To such an extent is this principle rife in their minds that it has more than once found expression in our local legislatures.

Continuing, the white man asks, What is education doing for the negro ?   Is he more industrious, more moral, or more honest ?

That the masses in the British West Indian possessions have not shown any marked advancement along educational lines is due to the sparing manner in which it has been distributed, so as to be of no tangible benefit to the receivers.

The educated negro is every bit the equal of the white man in warfare, athletics, literature, diplomacy, law, or medical researches, and in every other walk of life ; and in support of my contention, it is only necessary to name such men as Dobbs, Toussaint-L'Ouverture, Coleridge Taylor, Douglas, Dunbar, Taylor, Johnson Reeves, Dumas, Blyden, the Haytians Maître

Leger (member of the Academical Society of International History of Paris), an authority on diplomatic law, and the medical *savant* Andian, who is a member of the Society of Exotic Pathology (one of the most exclusive medical societies in the world, which admits only renowned medical celebrities to its ranks), besides many other eminent specialists in France, England, and America.

To fair-minded persons the assertion that education is an enemy to the negro cannot pass unchallenged, but as the object of this book is not to agitate the negro question, I consider that the best way to treat the matter is to leave it strictly alone, and allow it to work out its own salvation.

Educate a man and he finds that he has an honour to protect; his morals are improved as a result; he looks upon his kind with uplifting thoughts; and, finally, you make of him a person fit for any society.

Neglect this *essential* and you make the reverse of him, and, through want of sheer intelligence, he drifts away into the criminal class, and is lost as far as this world is concerned.

The records will show that, for this very want of education, there have been more foul and brutal murders committed throughout the world than would have been otherwise, and that this state of affairs obtains very largely in the West Indies in proportion to the bulk of illiteracy.

There are some who contend that the educated

negro refuses to return to tilling the soil. This, however, depends entirely upon the class of education which he receives, and the aims which such instructions tend to convey to his mind. If his education fits him only to become a clerk, a teacher, or a preacher, he cannot be expected to be an agriculturist.

If, on the other hand, his daily education has been associated with agriculture—the soil and plant life—in connection with his general education, the pupil soon learns that the wealth of the world lies in mother earth, and that it is the secret of the upkeep of the man who wields the pen.

The system which had hitherto been applied to the educational methods in the British West Indian colonies was to impress upon the minds of the rising generation that there is no dignity in labour; and, indeed, up to the present day, the man who does manual labour in the West Indies is looked down upon as unfit for any society.

There is no denying the fact that the main purpose of our colonial masters, up to recent years, was to discourage the promotion and advancement of all local industries in the colonies, whenever they came in direct competition with exports from the mother country.

Thus it seems to have proved, at the beginning, somewhat beneficial in postponing for two centuries or more, special agricultural instructions until this late day—the situation having demanded a decided change of front, on account of the advent of the American refiners on the scene.

The desire at present, due to competition, is not to make merely producers but self-supporters also. This is indeed a rapid change of front.

The great bulk of raw materials intended for British manufacturers and refiners now finds its way into the American markets. This is causing considerable alarm among those who are accountable for our destiny.

The United States now sends us much of the *corn* and *rice* which we consume—products which, had they been developed on scientific agricultural methods a hundred years ago, would have been one of the mainstays of the British West Indies ; but in those days the bulk of the supplies came from British sources, hence there was no need to worry.

We hear in these days glowing reports of what these colonies are able to produce for home consumption, and we trust that it is not too late to mend ; but why is it that even the suggestion of the development of our food supply must come from the *West Indian Committee* in *far-away* London ? Is it because we are so impotent, blind, or dead to our own interest ? No, this cannot be so. The cause lies at the bottom of the system of government under which the West Indian possessions of Great Britain are run, and until it is broken and a free and liberal institution set up in its stead for the people, so long will our energies lie dormant.

This " change of front " of our masters, in endeavouring to stimulate local self-supporting industries, is necessitated, as I have already stated, on account of the drift of raw materials, destined to furnish labour for the British working class in the opposite direction.

Great Britain finds to her discomfort that of the £7,000,000 worth of sugar produced in her West Indian possessions during 1897–98, only £1,500,000 of that amount found its way into the hands of her home refiners, the bulk going to the markets of the United States and other countries, and latterly some goodly portion to Canada.

This the English people permit for the want of better treatment to the West Indies, and in the interest of the ever-loving *free trade*, notwithstanding that her yearly consumption in this single commodity amounts to nothing less than £20,000,000.

It cannot be denied that if preference on sugar were granted to the West Indian colonies, to them would fall the pleasurable task of supplying the British markets with the greater portion of the sugar they need for home consumption, which would mean a big thing for these colonies—but the reverse is what has happened.

CHAPTER XVIII

THE nearest approach in the United Kingdom to a general military education began in the eighties, when James Smith of Glasgow, in the year 1883, organized the *boys' brigade,* which soon spread rapidly to the colonies.

In the United States of America, the system has been greatly improved upon. Here the members of a similar organization take on the title of *school cadets* possibly as a more fitting name from the American military point of view.

It provides that after a boy has passed through the lower grades of the elementary public schools, where he receives his preliminary education, and enters the high school, he dons a military uniform which consists of a close-fitting jacket and pants, made of regulation cloth, to which are added the necessary stripes and shoulder straps denoting the rank of the commissioned and non-commissioned officers, the privates being without, as the case warrants. This system also pertains to private schools and seminaries all over the country.

All scholars are enlisted as privates, and their subsequent advancement depends on their military studies, as well as their work and general deportment in the class-room and on the parade grounds.

It is most astonishing to mark the change which these military instructions, assisted by these smart-looking clothes, readily make in a lad. The boy who leaves the graded schools in a somewhat uncertain manner finds his whole life brightened up by this new regime, which, it if does nothing else, makes him physically a better man than he would otherwise have been.

In a few months one finds what was hitherto a humped, slouchy-moving lump of humanity, transformed into a new creature. His steps are much quicker, he assumes a military air, and moves along with a decided gait.

Whether in the class-room, on the streets, or on parade, he has foremost in his mind his obedience to his superior officer, and ultimately he is made into a soldier although a student, ready and fit to bear arms in the defence of the *Union*.

This amply accounts for the reason why the American private and the volunteer soldier are looked upon as the most intelligent mass of fighting men which, with the exception of the Germans and the Japanese, is found among the recruits of no other country.

In the United States it has been found that boys so trained, after leaving the high school, and the officers of these cadet corps have been sufficiently well equipped to officer volunteer corps and to be marched off, at a moment's notice, to the front.

During the Spanish-American war, many of these lads, both *coloured* and *white*, served with distinction, going directly from the class-room to the field.

Some few, after completing their course in the high school, have, with but very little extra preparation, gone up for the regular army with success and very favourable marks to their credit; which goes to prove that the system is by no means a toy affair, but in reality a compulsory military education in disguise, which has the decided advantage of developing the physique of the individual.

I have personal knowledge of several coloured youths who held the commission of first lieutenant in the High School Cadet Corps, and who enlisted in the volunteer service during the Spanish-American war, holding the same commission from the Secretary of War for the United States of America.

There was one young man who, after being mustered out at the close of the war, enlisted in the regular army as a private, and in six months he was promoted to the rank of sergeant-major, and within a year from the date of his enlistment, he sat for an examination for promotion to a commissioned officer and passed with credit.

The division commander and officers who had watched him daily, from the date of his enlistment as a private to that on which he received his shoulder-straps as second lieutenant in the regular army, endorsed his papers in the following terms, viz., that the young man in question was the " most perfect soldier that had ever passed under their notice."

Under the scheme of *federation* with *colonial self-government*, such a course inaugurated in connection with what is already being done on similar lines at present in most of the West Indian colonies, for at least five years, would furnish a most desirable class of youngsters for our volunteer corps and national police force.

The young men of to-day should be taught to handle the rifle at as early an age as is consistent with physical development. Judging from the signs of the time, education in these days must necessarily be extended farther than the use of the pen—it must also embody the use of the sword and rifle.

The evil of being enslaved or subjugated by a conquering foe, without the means of putting up a defence on behalf of one's self and home, is far more fearful than the *bogey* of militarism.

It would be unmistakably laid down in the constitution of the *United West Indies* that every male citizen must pay for the privilege of being a member of the world-wide Empire, by demonstrating his ability to serve in the defence of the federation and the Empire generally.

The opponents of militarism will readily denounce the idea of making every nook and corner of the British Empire an armed camp, as dangerous and unnecessary, but those who have been watching the warlike preparations of the great nations have been forced, by passing events, to come to the conclusion that war or bankruptcy is inevitable unless some arrangements can be entered into whereby a limitation of armaments can be agreed upon. This can hardly be accomplished, as every nation must decide, according to its aims, ambition, and ability to finance its offensive and defensive schemes, what is most needed for its preservation. Already Germany has thrown down the gauntlet that she wants no compromise, and that peace must be dearly bought.

It is the universal conclusion of those who are in a position to judge, that in the next great war the *Occident* will adopt the tactics of the *Orient*, and that, following the example of Japan when she launched herself against Russia, there will be no declaration of war in the next great conflict among civilized nations.

It will come upon us like a peal of thunder from a cloudless sky ; and with this knowledge it behoves us to begin to make preparations to face the issue, for those who aim at victory, where the forces are equally matched or nearly so, must strike the first blow at a vital spot without hesitation or warning.

The federated West Indies, with a population approaching 3,000,000 souls, will within a short time be able to provide a force of at least 800,000 men of all arms and branches of the service, which would be a force, when properly drilled and equipped, not to be easily despised.

About 95 per cent. of this force would be composed of men of the negro race, who, whatever their shortcomings may be, have always proved themselves excellent and brave soldiers, ready to risk their lives for the good of the service.

The British, French, and Americans can offer numerous examples of the grit and bravery of negro troops on the battlefield.

It was with the assistance of negro troops that the northerners were able to preserve the Union, in the great civil war waged in America between the north and the south.

They did it again in Cuba during the Spanish-American War when they won the day for the American flag, saved the rough-riders from total annihilation, and made Roosevelt president, while white soldiers shivered, faltered, and fell back before the Spanish riflemen.

In no case, under the French, English, or American flag, has he earned the title of "shirker" when some one was needed to step into the breach; and in this and every other respect he is the equal of any *soldier* that has ever shouldered a rifle, in the defence of a just cause, or in the *pillage* of weaker nations.

They were with Kitchener in the Soudan when he avenged the death of "Chinese Gordon," and greatly contributed to his success against the forces of the Mad Mullah.

In an editorial of the Trinidad *Mirror*, a daily paper published at Port of Spain, Trinidad, already referred to, dated March 19, 1910, "The necessities and superfluities of Trinidad Police Force," the editor ridiculed the idea that the police force of that island could be expected to make a stand against an invading foe, and hold out until help comes. He decried the idea of militarism which the authorities are infusing in the local police force as a waste of time, and he further intimated that the constabulary as a military guard is totally incapable.

One would like to think that he arrived at this conclusion on the basis of insufficient numbers or inefficiency of the management to fit these guardians of the peace for a double purpose, but, upon perusal of his article, it could be easily discerned that he desired to acquit the commanders of the force from all blame, and to condemn the personnel of the force as cowards, who would take to the woods at the first sight of an invading foe.

This he editorially suggested with the knowledge of the fact that many of the men composing the police force of Trinidad are discharged soldiers of the famous West Indian Regiment who have seen service and have proved themselves worthy of being entrusted with the honour and dignity of the British nation, while, on the other hand, the majority of these officers are men who have never been put to the test ; yet these latter are accredited with the bravery, while tried men are condemned with the whole as lacking in courage.

Were it possible, in the emergency, to have the editor's convictions materialized, it would certainly be a calamity to the British nation, and a blot upon the negro as a fighter, civilized or un-civilized.

Wendell Phillips, the great American orator, in his oration on Toussaint-L'Ouverture and in defence of the negro race, said :—" Some people read history with their eyes closed," and I add that it is patent that not a few write history with their consciences closed.

If the condemnation of the editor of the *Mirror* is true in the case of the Trinidad police force, then it must convey the same weight to the constabulary establishments throughout the West Indies.

We do not and cannot, in the face of abundance of facts to the contrary, accept his views as to the *yellow streak* in the negro as a fighting man.

CHAPTER XIX

THE WEST INDIAN NAVY

THE idea of a *West Indian Navy* would be a thing absolutely inconceivable were it not associated with federation of the British possessions in and about the Caribbean Sea, with colonial self-government.

Such a proposition could never have claimed serious thought under ordinary circumstances without provoking much laughter and ridicule from those familiar with the finances of the British West Indian possessions, the pauperized condition of the people, the present heavy and ever-increasing burden of taxation with which they are saddled, and the *general* dissatisfaction underlying the present system of government maintained in these colonies, where the *absolute power* is vested in a few, and the *will of the people*—the taxpayers —set at naught.

This system of colonial government, which every well-thinking West Indian disapproves of and condemns, as wholly unfit for an intelligent, law-abiding, God-fearing, and liberty-loving people, is the nearest approach to *Autocracy* by the British Government : a " system " more suited to a

Russian province than a British colony, the· property of a nation by whom liberty, of all other attributes, is held most sacred.

Have not the British spirit and love of liberty followed the flag to Australia, Canada, and South Africa ?   Then why not to the West Indies ?

The matter of a *West Indian Navy*, however, takes on a new phase and a more serious attitude when such a scheme is mentioned in connection with a union of the British West Indian possessions with *responsible government*.

With the positive assurance that the *Cuban* programme is to construct a *Dreadnought* and a fleet of ocean-going torpedo-boat destroyers, torpedo boats, and submarines, the suggestion that the United West Indies could and should have a navy worthy to be called upon in the defence of its native shores and the Empire, loses much of what would otherwise be termed ridiculousness on the part of the exponents of a West Indian naval organization.

When it is taken into consideration that the entire resources of Cuba, developed and undeveloped, can never hope to approximate the undeveloped resources of countries like British Guiana, Jamaica, Trinidad, and British Honduras, one can feel with a degree of certainty that the time will surely come when we too under *federation* and *self-government* may with pride look forward to a Navy as a protection for our native land, and as a further means of strengthening the influence of the *mother country* in the Caribbean Sea.

Mr. Richard Jebb, writing in The Standard, a London paper, on the subject of " The West Indies and the Empire," expresses his views as to what he considers would be the right policy for restoring and consolidating the British Power in the West Indies as follows :—

" The Federation of the Colonies which is economically necessary in any case, would lend itself also to a union for naval defence : the West Indies themselves replacing the vanished instrument of British sea power in these parts.

" A naval squadron corresponding in principles to the West Indian Regiment would appeal strongly to the sentiments of the negroes, who would submit cheerfully to special taxation for the purpose.

" The squadron should be manned as far as possible by the islanders themselves, many of whom are born seamen, and the ships supplied to begin with by the Imperial government should be maintained out of the joint West Indian Revenue, which might be expected to increase rapidly under Imperial preferential stimulus.

" This new link between the islands, coupled with improved mail service and inter-colonial Free Trade, would enlarge the political outlook of the people, tending to expand a parochial into a West Indian patriotism.

" The present gravitation towards the United States would be counteracted, not only for the British, but also for the other islands, by a new centre of attraction in a vigorous Caribbean Confederation under the British flag inspired with the sense of a future political welfare full of possibilities."

Mr. Jebb is wrong in his conclusion that " the negro (of the West Indies) would cheerfully submit to special taxation," for the glory of a West Indian Navy, and while it is not expected that they would depart from their usual humble and cowering demeanour, by making a popular and forcible demonstration against any additional taxation to this end, yet the word " cheerfully " is entirely out of the question.

That they would be forced to *submit* in the face of opposing forces, against which they are powerless to contend, is too true, but to anticipate intelligent beings as accepting such a situation " cheerfully " is an insult to the average West Indian.

What may be said of the future of a West Indian navy amounts to but very little, since every native of the West Indies realizes that such a force could never hope independently to adopt an offensive or defensive position against any of the great conquering nations for many scores of years to come, without facing instant destruction.

Consequently they are made to appreciate the position that such an organization could only be of use as an adjunct to the great Imperial Navy, serving as a link to complete the chain which is to bind the greatest of Empires in modern times inseparably together.

Such a naval force, therefore, would be primarily for assisting in preserving in these parts the territory of this greatest of Empires, and, as a consequent secondary result, the protection of the natives of these West Indian possessions, which go with the territory.

We realize that the federation of the British West Indian possessions, *without* colonial self-government, would be the placing of double-edged weapons in the hands of our *Official Masters*, namely " The West Indian Committee," who, acting in conjunction with the " Colonial Office," dominate the West Indies ; thus signing our own death-warrant.

On the same grounds we also realize that a navy built under such conditions from the general funds of the Treasury would be very unpopular, unless the people are given a say in the matter. How then could Mr. Jebb expect us as rational beings to *submit cheerfully*, as he puts it ? Those who have lived under the British Crown Colony Government know that it is immaterial to protest against any high-handed action emanating from Downing Street.

The Colonial Office will continue to do as it pleases with the people and the money of all such possessions coming under its direction, without regard for the feelings of the inhabitants, when issues that are of *paramount importance* to this august department are to be carried out, be they right or wrong.

What we should be most careful about, since we cannot stay the hand that wields the sword, is to refrain from inviting extra burdens upon our heads, under the popular guise of loyalty.

Perhaps this gentleman has in his mind a

further plan of salvation in connection with his ideas on Federation of the West Indies, which he, like other members of the white race, is loth to extend to negroes and persons of negro origin, namely, "Responsible Government," which would give every native son of the soil an opportunity to participate in the management of the affairs of the land of his birth. It is only under such conditions that the inhabitants of the British West Indian possessions would *submit cheerfully to extra taxation* for the construction and maintenance of the West Indian Navy.

In such an organization, the opportunity for the unrestricted advancement of natives from one grade to the other would most certainly have to be of vastly wider scope than those which are now opened to them in the *crack regiment* (West Indian Regiment), from which he draws an analogy.

The principle of equal privileges, as applied to Englishmen in England and throughout the self-governing colonies, would also be rigidly applied with reference to any future military or naval establishments for the West Indies, under the proposed new regime (Federation, with Responsible Government).

The verdict would no longer be, Because thou art a negro, thus far shalt thou go and no farther —on the contrary, every promotion in the rank and file would be opened to unrestricted competition to every British subject qualified to compete; therefore without regard to colour, creed, race, or previous standing. Qualification, in the broad sense of the word, would be the watchword and the only road to promotion.

Our native soldiery and police force which, under the present management, are looked down upon, in contrast to similar organizations in other countries, for the subserviency which is required of the men who join them would at once assume a more dignified stand, from the fact that native sons, of education and refinement, would be attracted thereto, seeing that *iniquitous barrier* to their unrestricted promotion is unreservedly removed.

All that a West Indian negro wants is a fair and untrammelled opportunity to exist in the land of his birth. He does not ask for favours at the hands of his bondsmen.

When Mr. Jebb touched upon the subject of *Imperial preferential treatment* for the West Indies he touched directly upon the keynote of the prosperity of these colonies, when it is taken into consideration that Great Britain imports £20,000,000 worth of sugar annually, which is one of the chief products of her West Indian possessions.

It is therefore evident that, if we were granted preference, *even on this single item*, it would mean that we should be thereby assisted in furnishing the larger portion of this article to the British consumers.

*Cane-farming,** which in places like Trinidad

* Cane-farming consists of cane grown by small settlers and sold to the estate and central factories, as against cane grown on the estate proper.

constitutes one-third of the total cane harvest,
would progress by leaps and bounds. Estates
would be in a far better position to engage *free
labour* as against the present slave trade, now
carried on with the consent of the Colonial Office
and West Indian Committee, in coolie importation
for *specified time and specific purpose*.

Capitalists would readily invest their money in
existing sugar estates, by opening new ones, making
loans, etc., feeling certain that the industry has
substantial backing in preferential treatment from
the mother country, and the final results would
be an awakening of the comparatively dormant
industries, from which men of the past accumulated such vast wealth that it is said of one :
On returning to England from the West Indies,
he shod his horse with golden shoes and rode
him through the streets of London, as a demonstration of the great wealth that was to be made
in these colonies in those days when *sugar was
king*.

Confederation of the British West Indian
colonies, with self-government, reorganization, retrenchment, and imperial preferential treatment,
would go a long way towards relieving the present
stagnant state of affairs in these His Majesty's
possessions, wherein oppressive measures and
starvation form at present the order of the day.

It would appear, however, that, in spite of our
urgent appeals and wants, nothing will be done
for us in the matter of *preferential treatment*
from the mother country so long as she remains

wedded to the policy of *free trade*. After the
abolition of slavery in the British West Indies,
notwithstanding that the planters had to produce
their sugar with paid labour as against that produced by countries which still owned slaves, the
Home Government refused to grant *preference* on
the sugar coming in from the Colonies. As a result, the sugar produced by slave labour was able
to undersell that produced by paid labour, and
that was the first telling blow administered to
the West Indian sugar trade. The fall in production was due to the laziness of the negroes as
some suppose; and, as proof against this calumnious
assertion, I have only to point to Cuba, which produces more than twice the quantity of sugar produced by any other one country in the world with
negro labour. They do not import coolies, but,
instead of this, they pay the natives well for their
labour. Judging from such a severe object-lesson
in the interest of *free trade* which England's foremost statesmen of the present day declare is vital
to the life of the British workmen, I fear that
the change for which we are hoping will never
come. We must still hope on, nevertheless, that
in the near future circumstances may be so
changed as to clear the way for the granting of
this much-needed *preference* on the products of the
British West Indies going into English markets.

In such an event, not only would an attempt
be made to send her all, or the greater quantity, of
the sugar necessary for home consumption, but
under the *stimulus* a still greater effort would be

made to send her some of the many million
bunches of bananas, which she now gets from the
Canaries, in place of the few thousands which we
now send.

I quite agree with Mr. Jebb that, under federation, intercolonial free trade could be developed
to a very great extent, as, according to the Colonial
Office List of 1910, *intercolonial commerce* of
the previous year amounted to over £2,500,000,
and this in opposition to the obstacles placed by
one colony in the path of the other, to the
hindrance of this very commerce.

We on this side, unlike Mr. Jebb, are of the
opinion that there can be no general confederation
of the islands in the Caribbean Sea *under the
British* flag, for to have this done the islands
which are now sovereign states, or practically
so, would necessarily have to surrender their
sovereignty according to his scheme, which none
of us would live long enough to see.

The people who have tasted freedom would
never tamely submit to British rule as it is meted
out to her Crown Colonies.   What influence
responsible government for the British West
Indies will have upon these neighbouring islands is
another question, providing, however, the influence
of America can be eliminated.

It must be remembered that if, even beyond our
wildest imaginations, Cuba, Hayti, and San Domingo decide to join hands with us as British
self-governing colonies, there are certain obstacles
which would have to be overcome, the chief

among them being the opposition which would come from the United States, on the plea of endangering the life of the much cherished *Monroe Doctrine*.

In conjunction with what has already been said with reference to the establishment of a West Indian Navy on liberal lines, we would most likely pursue quite a different course from that which is contemplated by Cuba.

What we should need in such a case would be swift protected cruisers of the *Bona Ventura* class, torpedo-boat destroyers, torpedo and submarine boats, in sufficient numbers, distributed throughout the confederacy to guard our coasts and harbours. That would be the programme for the beginning; if the future created the necessity for larger ships it would be time then to decide, but the present needs would be the first to receive attention.

The estimated cost of four cruisers of the class mentioned, equipped and ready for service, would be about £1,000,000, and would call for not less than 3,000 officers and men to man them.

The cost of these warships, added to torpedo boats, submarines, and torpedo-boat destroyers, when armed and manned, would make the sum total run up to £2,000,000, plus the cost of maintenance.

There being no naval unit in the West Indies, the majority of the crew and all the officers, to begin with, would be loaned by the Imperial Naval Board, to be gradually replaced by native officers and men, as soon as these are trained to take up their respective stations. As coloured men are not permitted to enter the Naval and Military academies of England, through popular sentiment, it would be found necessary to have built in the colonies an institution for the training of our naval men, for which a capable and experienced staff of instructors would be engaged permanently from the mother country.

The ships having been loaned to form the nucleus, as Mr. Jebb suggests, while the new navy is being constructed, manned, and equipped, there remains only the question of finances to defray the current expenses of running the concern, which could be reasonably obtained under reorganization and retrenchment, as already suggested.

In Canada a section of the people, guided by American sentiment which for some deep-seated reason is opposed to Canada's naval policy, are ready to question as to who shall have the right to declare war in the presence of a Canadian Navy, and intimated that, if the Dominion is to be drawn into any conflict which is Britain's policy to prosecute, the cause should be fully made known to the Dominion parliament, so that she may be in a position to decide whether it would be to Canada's interest or not to participate therein. As far as our military aspirations are concerned, it would be proposed to increase our present police force into a national guard, properly drilled and equipped. These would serve as guardians of the peace in times of tranquillity and as soldiers in times of hostility.

Happily, the American feeling referred to above is not unanimous in Canada, or else it would look gloomy for England, and this can never be, for there are many (Canadians) who still fully realize that, comparing the Dominion with other powers with naval and military aspirations, she is very much in the embryonic stage, and may possibly remain in her infancy for half a century yet to come.   In such a case it would be dangerous to leave the convoy and venture out alone in troubled waters.

The policy of the Navy of the United West Indies would not be guided by such sentiments. We do not maintain that we are more loyal than the Canadians, but, nevertheless, we would stand by the policy of *The Three Musketeers* in Dumas' famous novel—" All for one and one for all,"— or the whole Empire or none.

Every French subject is a Frenchman ; why is not every British subject a Britisher ?

CHAPTER XX

LOYALTY OF THE SELF-GOVERNING COLONIES

WE view with constant alarm the spirit often displayed by those who are, in a measure, responsible for the destiny of Great Britain, by the indifference which they manifest towards some of her colonies.

Let us take the small but important matter of the British Colonial mails, which were carried from Jamaica to Central America on German ships, beginning during the year 1909.

It will be found that these mails were formerly transported by the Royal Mail Steam Packet Co., but, owing to the curtailing of a few pennies on the gross weight of this *matter*, as a means of retrenchment by the island's government, a British steamship company refused to do the carrying for a price which is very readily accepted by the ships of a company of a rival nation—the Hamburg-American line—a German concern.

For the same reason of splitting hairs with the West Indian colonies by British steamship companies, we find to our astonishment that freight can be carried from England to Australia at a much cheaper rate than to the West Indies.

The long-hoped-for United Empire, the dream of Mr. Joseph Chamberlain, of Boer War fame, can only be an accomplished fact when all her colonies are made self-governing.

There can be no *halfway*, no substitution for the reality ; this is the *one course* without an alternative, and it must be adopted swiftly to be effective. Delay is dangerous, and as the tempest is gathering on the horizon we must " make hay while the sun shines."

The paramount and most natural feeling among the greatest minds of the great self-governing colonies, a feeling which would be re-echoed by the United West Indies, is that they are bound by the most sacred ties to prosecute *any policy* which the mother country chooses to adopt for the preservation of her sovereignty as the world's greatest power.

Right or wrong, her cause must be our cause ; her burdens our burdens ; her wars our wars, even if such a conflict must be waged against a disloyal daughter, self-governing colony, who gets it into her head that she can withdraw from the union of the empire at her own discretion.

In such a case, as in every other that would follow, if necessary, the rest of the empire would go forth to chastise the truant member of the family and bring her back to the union. A Roberts would be found to reconquer South Africa ; a Wolfe to retake Quebec, if it is the command of the mother country that the union shall not be disrupted.

I cannot agree with the views of Mr. F. D. Monk, of Canada, that the Dominion would be better served if she spent her money on the development of her transportation facilities, rather than in making a sacrifice to set aside an appropriate sum for the construction and maintenance of a navy in aid of the Imperial Defence Scheme.

Mr. Monk, in his article, deplores the idea of the *Dominion mixing up with the miseries, foolish quarrels*, and grave problems which Europe presents.

He evidently has not taken the right view, in my opinion, of the relationship which exists between the mother country and the self-governing colonies.

Apart from any political ties, there exists between the self-governing colonies and the mother country the true relation of mother and daughter; and until Canada is able to hoist her flag of *absolute independence* this relationship must inevitably continue.

In view of this *fact*, how is it possible for the child to say to its mother : " I am unable to mix up with your miseries and troubles," when the very existence of that mother is seriously imperilled ? Impossible ! Impossible ! !   Such a child would be unworthy of a parent.

It is good that we realize that politics and patriotism are two separate and distinct questions which bear no relationship, and consequently must not be confounded one with the other, or else one would be forced to take the assertions of

Mr. Monk with some seriousness, and brand him as unpatriotic and ungrateful.

Most certainly no member of the United Empire would concern himself with the *grave problems which Europe presents*, if they did not threaten British sovereignty and endanger the existence of the British Isles and of Greater Britain beyond the seas.

Far-seeing Canadians are fully cognizant of the fact that the fall of Great Britain would mean the death of Canada's ambition one day to become an independent nation.

The *Quebec Chronicle* throws down the gauntlet to those in whose hands the administration of the Dominion's affairs is entrusted when it says :—

" In plain English the declaration of the Premier means that, if Canada decides to remain neutral in the war, she must lower the British flag and become independent."

These are Canada's answers to America's efforts to discourage a Canadian naval policy, and a warning to Germany that it must be *the whole hog or none*.

Could such loyalty have come from a subjugated people ? Could people who are kept down by a system of Crown Colony Government, or outnumbered by nominated officials in a *farce legislature*, have seriously expressed themselves in such loyal terms as those of the *Premier* regarding the future policy of the Dominion ? Never ! Never ! !

Taxation without representation is an institution long extinct in Canada, because no white race, no matter what the consequences, would long stand for such an imposition ; and that is the reason why we have a Canadian navy, in the asking, to-day.

If the present relationship between the mother country and the Dominion were to be broken, the latter assuming all the responsibility of government, she would soon find to her own sorrows that the much-vaunted *Monroe Doctrine* would be no protection for her, as some Canadians suppose, against a country like Germany, which breathes *living fires* at the very mention of the *term* ; a policy which all Germans characterize as a *piece of impertinence* on the part of a young nation like America.

If we allow, for the sake of argument, that Canada had refused to contribute to the Imperial Defence Scheme, putting her whole trust in the all-powerful Monroe Doctrine, and in the meantime Germany swoops down on England overnight, keeps Britain's fleet occupied in home waters while she despatches fast and powerful cruisers of the *Invincible* type to harass Canadian ports and destroy her shipping : where would the Dominion find herself in such a crisis ?

Of course, this would afford the glorious opportunity for which the Americans are ever on the look-out, to come in with their *Monroe Doctrine* and say, " Leave it to us; we have a powerful modern navy, a standing army, and a large population from which to draw volunteers; we will protect you." As this protection would not be effective unless American troops were moved to Canadian soil and her navy to Canada's waters, it would be found necessary to establish several working bases on the territory of the Dominion, in order to assist more efficiently in repelling the invasion.

The cost of such a protection, which would be enormous, would most naturally fall on the Dominion's treasury, and, taking opportunity of her depletion after such a war, the United States would continue to occupy the chief seaports until the last dollar was paid.

This is a condition of affairs which every well thinking Canadian desires to avoid, as it would mean the instalment of American control over the destinies of the Dominion, and a consequent passing of her self-governing powers.

Luckily, the anti-naval party was in a hopeless minority, and as such did not triumph. The result is that Canada is to have a navy, which we hope will in a short time after its inauguration be in a position to assume the *offensive* and *defensive*, without the aid of her perilous neighbour.

In making this charge against the great American nation of being a *land grabber*, as bad as any European nation, it is not my purpose to hold myself up as a paragon of honest intention while denouncing other persons as dishonest: far from it. My conclusions are merely deductions from the *tide* in which all conquering nations irresistibly drift, sooner or later, and of which there are many striking illustrations to bear out my contentions.

I have seen sufficient examples of America's proffered help, which has been so unwittingly and innocently accepted on such occasions.

A most striking illustration is found in the case of the Philippines, where glittering promises of protection and independent government were held out to General Aguinaldo by American representatives, on the eve of the destruction of the *timber-built* ships of Spain, at the naval Battle of the Sea of Manila.

The Republic of Panama can also say something about the tentacles of the *Monroe Doctrine* when she, without army or navy, found herself opposed by Colombia, and accepted the apparently harmless help extended to her by the wily Yankees.

America's help to Canada in a position where the latter is unable to defend herself against an invader, would be the case of Japan in Manchuria all over again, where the *friend* promptly becomes the *foe*.

Another point in order of reasonable discussion would be the hoisting of the American flag on Canadian merchantmen, in the event of England being unable to give the Dominion naval assistance through unfortunate circumstances occurring on the other side.

Under such circumstances it would be seen that, in the course of a year or more, while the battle rages on sea and land, the Americans would so firmly entrench themselves on Canadian soil, that it would take something more forcible than ordinary diplomatic persuasion to dislodge them at the close of the war.

With a fleet of mighty warships in Canadian harbours, their base strongly fortified, a mighty army of volunteers ready to step over the line into the territory of the Dominion at the first sign of resistance, the Canadians would find themselves in an awful predicament.

It would be too late then to reflect upon the golden opportunities which were offered to the Dominion to provide a navy for her own defence, for the American flag once hoisted on Canadian soil would be there to stay.

It is to Canada's interest, therefore, to let the *Monroe Doctrine*, with its divergent aims, strictly alone, as an element of extreme uncertainty fraught with many evils.

Quite fortunately for Canada, the better judgment of her foremost politicians has prevailed, and it is to be hoped that now the hands are set to the plough, there will be no looking back until the Canadian naval flag shall have become an emblem of respect the world over.

If the empire of Great Britain is to exist another quarter of a century, the self-governing colonies must stand together as a unit and, to use the exact words of the *Ottawa Citizen*—a Canadian daily paper—on the Dominion's attitude :

" It is a gratuitous piece of offensiveness to proclaim that Canada reserves the right to repudiate the claim of Great Britain to its support, lest the mother country should drag Canada into some disgraceful international broil."

This assertion is evidently intended for persons who share in Mr. Monk's opinion, relative to the stand which Canada should take in the Imperial Defence Scheme.

This *scheme* as far as it is connected with the colonies is primarily intended to relieve the Imperial Fleet proper from doing coast defence duty thousands of miles away from its main base, to protect the commerce of the colonies and, as a last resort, to go in aid of the mother country whenever such a course becomes necessary.

Its purpose is not directed at having the colonies mixed up unnecessarily in European broils, or to have them decide on the issue at stake that they are reminded of their defenceless position, but for their own security and salvation as self-governing colonies.

While the confederation of the British West Indies with a broad and liberal form of government is of paramount importance, it must be borne in mind that the one without *the other* would be positively undesirable.

Crown Colony Government at its best is a government of subjugation, under which the people are semi-slaves ; and in consequence of such a condition we would never presume, as long as this system of government is maintained, to look upon ourselves as constituting a part of the British Empire, which stands for freedom in every sense of the word.

When will this change come about, so that the inhabitants of these colonies can with a clear conscience number themselves as forming part and parcel of this great union of the Empire ?

That is the question which is every day being asked by press and public.   We have asked aloud but no answer came save the echo of our own voices, and now we have begun to knock at the door of liberty in real earnest ; will it be opened unto us or not ?   The Scriptures, in Matthew viii. 7, 8, assure us that " Every one that asketh receiveth, and he that seeketh findeth, and unto him that knocketh it shall be opened."   We hope and wait.

To-day " we are standing on the threshold of a new decade " as certain as we break the bread of life.   We are being guided by an administration in the mother country which is fair and liberal in all its deliberations.   We are being ruled by a sovereign who, we are certain, will exert his influence for the relief of every distress, so far as lies in his power, among his many millions of subjects.

Should we not be hopeful that the end of the present pernicious system of government is fast approaching ?

The time for self-government for the West Indian colonies of Great Britain is at hand, and if the opportunity is not acted upon without delay, we are certain to be overtaken by disaster and these possessions will be lost to the British Empire.

If we instruct ourselves while there is yet time, we may be able to avert the calamity which under the present circumstances seems inevitable. The " inevitable " to which I refer is none other than the approaching Anglo-German war, which is bound to come about, unless one of the two nations decides to step down as a means of avoiding national bankruptcy.

The contesting nations in naval armament have made their respective positions clear before the world and that is : Each will pursue a policy of its own in keeping with its national demands— the final result of which will be war. It is with respect to this *end* that we wish to prepare ourselves to the fullest.

It is the most sanguine desire of the coloured and black people, who constitute the bulk of the inhabitants of these colonies, in spite of all gloomy forebodings, to seek to preserve a spot on earth where persons of a negro race may find a haven of rest ; and the place chosen for this asylum is the land of their birth, to which they have a natural claim beyond the shadow of a doubt.

Now that we have presumed to be able to take care of ourselves and of our affairs, it remains only for us to be given an opportunity to demonstrate our ability to carry on the government as we suppose we can, and so take our stand in the ranks of self-governing colonies.

There are many who, having become wedded to Crown Government, will say that the propositions set out in this book are unwarranted ; but, in spite of such opposition, the fact remains that 99 per cent. of the total population of these colonies are for responsible government.

This great desire to be unshackled by a latent and obsolete form of government is by nature the heritage of the West Indians, surrounded as they are on every side by self-governing states, all of which are making rapid strides ahead, while we are being hopelessly outdistanced.

CHAPTER XXI

THE QUESTION OF REVENUE

WHEN the United West Indies—which union must come sooner or later—starts out on her self-governing policy, she will find herself confronted (allowing for natural fluctuations) with a national debt of about £7,000,000, a population fast approaching 3,000,000 souls, an export trade of over £10,350,000, an annual expenditure of £3,174,627, a revenue of £3,114,044, a conjointed territory (excluding Bermudas) of 110,827 square miles, twice as large as England and Wales, and capable of maintaining a population of 40,000,000. I put it that the expected change in the administration of these colonies will not be delayed longer than another twenty years, and the increase or decrease for that period in the general summary will not vary materially from the figures recorded herein.

If, however, our ideal was to be realized at this very moment, it would meet us with a deficit of over £60,000 on the finances of the union, which would at a glance make matters look extremely gloomy for our navy and increased national police force, were it not shown that there is ample and abundant room for retrenchment under re-organization.

Of course, there are some taxes that could be imposed in conjunction with retrenchment to assist our military and naval scheme, such as *income tax, increased legacy tax.*

We suggest the abolition of the house tax and the institution of a poll tax, together with the increase of the liquor licence to at least £30,000 per annum ; but no general and extensive plan of taxation which would add any extra weight to the already over-burdened peasant ratepayers.

The increase in tax on the sale of spirits would not in any way affect the revenue ; on the contrary, it would, though tending to lessen the number of loathsome rum-shops, which are now found at every corner in some of our cities, bring in more cash while promoting a healthier condition in the bar-rooms.

For instance, on the Canal Zone Strip, Republic of Panama, there were in 1910 fifty-six (56) licences to sell spirituous liquors issued at £240 each, showing an income of over £13,000. I doubt whether in places like Jamaica, where rum-shops are to be found at every angle, the Government derives anything like the amount of revenue from this source paid to the Canal Zone Government over the same area.

Such a scheme would also tend to lessen drunkenness, murder, assaults, and such crimes as have their direct bearing on the drinking of rum.

In Trinidad, where the licence for the sale of intoxicants is £200 for the chief cities and £100 for the lesser ones, drunkards do not number one in ten thousand, and the class of bar-rooms is of such a standard that no one need be ashamed of them.

The mother country being our only creditor, it would be safe to say that she would, in such an event, cancel our entire indebtedness to her as an encouragement to our new venture, and relieve the new administration of what would undoubtedly prove a great embarrassment.

That item having been overcome, the battle royal would begin in real earnest to find the means, if we aspire to a naval and military force to carry out our programme, before the first thing towards it could be done.

I have already pointed out that, according to figures at hand, there is a deficit in general revenue when this is tallied against the expenditure, together with the inexpediency of imposing any general and extensive form of additional taxation that would tend to increase the already heavy burden of the peasantry.

If this objection is upheld, to overcome the great obstacle of a total lack of finance to carry out our plans it would be necessary to reorganize the local governments coming under the con-federacy, and run them upon an economical basis.

As soon as this is accomplished we could with certainty go a-borrowing, feeling sure that we should soon have in our possession the means to

repay such loans and all interest incurred in conjunction therewith.

This conclusion is arrived at from the fact that
under the redistribution scheme, which I shall
submit herein, we should be able to save a matter
of £16,517 out of the total sum of £33,867 now
paid for the services of governors, their secretaries,
colonial secretaries, and their assistants in the
various West Indian colonies, while the men under
the new regime would not suffer in the least, as
they would receive salaries equivalent to those
paid for the same services in Canada and the
United States, Australia, Great Britain, France,
and Germany.

Besides the above, it is estimated on the whole,
that, out of our national expenditure of $3\frac{1}{8}$ million
pounds sterling, fully £2,000,000 annually could
under confederation and retrenchment be saved
according to the present calculations.

The resources of the United West Indies,
which are at present awaiting development, more
especially in colonies like British Guiana, Trinidad, Jamaica, and British Honduras, are numerous and productive : quite capable of putting us
upon a substantial footing.

Apart from the minerals, which are shown to be
existing in paying quantities in many of these
colonies, it goes without saying that the soil is
abundantly fertile, capable of supplying every
form of product except those which are purely
indigenous to the temperate zones.

Our fruit and other minor industries are capable

of enormous possibilities when placed in the hands of a government which is directly interested, heart and soul, instead of being run by an administration which is solely dependent on the advice of parties, whose interes it is to keep the West Indies in the background as long as possible, so that they may continue in the hands of the sacred few.

Twenty years ago it would have been considered preposterous to presume to suggest a union of these colonies with responsible government and the manner in which such an administration should be conducted.

Ten years later it would have been considered less so, and to-day the suggestion is quite within the range of practical politics.

This has been made possible by the puny change in the policy of the Home Government towards the colonies, and by the chain of surrounding circumstances.

We feel that in our present sovereign, King George V., we have a man of the broadest possible ideas, who knows the West Indies—not in the manner of Froude, Hall Caine, or the West Indian Committee, the tactical enemies of these possessions, whose opinions in the past governed the acts of his predecessors—but from his personal knowledge, having been among them, and having come in contact with a most representative section of the inhabitants of these colonies.

In Jamaica he opened an exhibition, saw the people, talked with some, and is therefore in a better position to determine for the Colonial Office, than it for him, whenever the destinies and future welfare of these possessions are being weighed, as they are at this moment.

There is abundant hope, therefore, that His Gracious Majesty will listen to our appeal for responsible government, and do everything that is in his power to bring about for the West Indies a more satisfactory state of government than that under which we are now labouring.

I venture to say that the form of *Liberal Government* which would be best suited for the West Indies is not such a difficult matter to settle, if those to whose hands the laying of the foundation is intrusted are allowed a free hand, without any attempt at bungling on the other side.

It is a known fact that, whenever any salvation of that character is to fall upon the West Indies, no matter how mild in character, the Colonial Office has always stepped in and deterred the agents of the Crown in these colonies from assuming the direct responsibility for such changes.

The majority of our local legislators, while the Crown holds aloof, naturally shrink from assuming the responsibility of doing that which, if proved unsuccessful, will reverse the clock of progress for another half a century : but let it be a mandate from the Colonial Secretary's office, as in cases when that office desires to have anything done, even against the will of the taxpayers, and see what would be the response.

This policy of *hide and seek* has had its desired

effect upon the people, who are constantly being reminded upon the slightest blunder that, " What the mother country can give, it can also take away."

The course which seems most feasible to suggest is that, when the government is ready to act, the several governors of the various possessions should be directed to have a conference and formulate plans for a national convention, and to summon to this gathering a certain number of representatives from the various islands according to the ratio of the population, to deliberate and confer with one another on the subject of the " best form of responsible government " that should be adopted.

This is the plan I would suggest as a preliminary move, and at this convention the governors of the various colonies protecting the interest of the Crown, the form of government and manner in which it ought to be administered, would be thoroughly threshed out and submitted for the approval of the Home Government.

It would be expected that, following the course of other representative governments, the constitution of the United West Indies would not differ materially from all others. In this connection we would therefore anticipate no trouble.

We should in the first place, for economical and other reasons, find the necessity of a Federal Parliament consisting of an upper and lower house ; the Governor-General of the union as President of the Council, with a salary of £5,000 per annum.

The Federal Parliament would convene once a year, for at least four months, to transact the business of the National Government, which would not have it in its power to override the law-making powers of the local governments of each colony, except when such laws encroach on the principles of the National Government.

For the purpose of economy the union would be divided into sections. Leeward Islands would be classed under Division " A," the Windward Islands under Division " B," each under the governorship of an administrator, with the title of Lieutenant-Governor and a salary of £1,800 annually.

Jamaica and its dependencies, Trinidad, and British Guiana, each occupying a distinctive division, " C," " D," " E," each governed by a lieutenant-governor, with salaries at £1,800 ; those of British Honduras and the Bahamas, including Turk's and Caicos Islands, under Divisions " F " and " G," receiving respectively £1,200 yearly, and a colonial secretary for each division.

Under this arrangement the government of the federation would be classed under eight divisions, with one governor-general and eight lieutenant-governors at a total cost of £18,200, with the addition of an extra £1,600 for secretaries of £200 each, making the whole amount £19,800 against the present cost £33,867, for governors, colonial secretaries, and their assistants.

I have shown in preceding statements that it is possible to save something over and above

£14,000 in one department alone—that of the executive, consisting of governors, colonial secretaries, and their assistants.

I shall also show that some savings could be accomplished in our department of Justice, as another example, leaving my readers to judge what can be ultimately accomplished, if retrenchment is carried along vigorously in all other departments under federation.

I reason that our Judicial Department could be run at a less cost, if the slave-traffic in coolie immigration, and the promiscuous sale of alcoholic liquors are discontinued, since these two evils furnish the pabulum for the generation of crimes; but at present I shall content myself with dealing with our chief justices, puisne judges, and attorney-generals.

The colonies which would come under the union at present boast of eleven chief justices, drawing salaries amounting to £11,425—five puisne judges, drawing £6,500, and nine attorney-generals at the cost of £7,780, with private practices, etc., making a total of £25,705 annually.

Under the confederation it would be found necessary to have but one chief justice of the Supreme Court of the Union at a salary of £2,000 per year, one attorney-general with a salary of £1,000, and two puisne judges at £1,000 each, as associate judges of the Supreme Court.

This arrangement would reduce the present cost by £20,000 in the Judicial Department. The places made vacant would be occupied by resident magistrates, with enlarged powers as circuit judges if it is found impossible to have the Supreme Court holding circuits annually in each division.

In cases of murder or appeals, three magistrates would sit to discharge such duties ; all appeals from their judgment would go to the Supreme Court of the Federal Government.

Enlarged powers in this case would not necessarily mean enlarged salaries, as at present some of these dignitaries receive the snug sum of £800 as salary and £200 travelling expenses, which is as much as the Chief Justice of the Supreme Court of the District of Columbia, Washington, D.C., U.S.A., receives for his services.

In this way it would be hoped that a substantial retrenchment could be shown from the salaries of twenty-six men of the present judicial system maintained in the West Indies, without doing any damage to the underman.

It is out of the question to argue that, if there was a wholesale reduction in staff and salaries in every department—which is economically necessary—we should find it difficult to get men to serve.

This is emphatically not so, since many capable local men could be found to fill all positions which are subordinate to that of the governor-general, without having to resort to the painful duty of importing them from abroad.

The nearest approach to the amount paid by these colonies to their officials is taken from the Colonial Office List of 1909, which shows a sum

total of over £370,000, not including municipa
officers, and the army of sub-employees comin;
under the various sub-branches of these depart
ments, while that of the Dominion of Canada
including nine Provinces and a Federal Government, is run at the sum of £280,000, a difference
of £90,000 against that of the West Indian
colonies.

When we think of the vastness of the wealth
of Canada—the Province of British Columbia
alone producing minerals in 1907 to the value of
£58,502,496—against the total revenue for the
West Indian colonies of £3,000,000—we are
compelled to ask how is this state of things
possible ? But facts are stubborn things, they
speak for themselves.

The solution of the mystery lies in the advantage of self-government, and there is nothing to
prevent us making a creditable showing when we
are placed on a similar footing.

Cuba was a bankrupt state for many scores of
years, a burden to Spain and to herself, but what
is her position to-day ? She shows an appreciable
surplus on her revenue of two or three million
dollars, which is another example of what can be
done under responsible government.

Many of these officials occupy two, sometimes
three offices, for which they draw salaries under
their several headings ; also fees, allowances,
quarters, actual and travelling expenses, the
average cost of which is not accounted for under
the head of disbursement of salaries.

One can readily realize what this disinterested policy has led up to, and the great and unnecessary all-round burden it throws upon the shoulders of the poor taxpayers, when it is known that the inefficient medical service of the Island of Trinidad claims the modest amount of £22,480 annually, of which sum over £19,000 is divided up among thirty-seven medical men, all of whom are allowed private practice, thirty-two of the number receiving in addition free quarters and other assistance; but that is not all, for the entire service, including hospitals, dispensaries, public health, and quarantine, amounts to £76,880.

The medical service of British Guiana figured at £30,890, with private practice, etc., but the total cost of running the medical department of the colony is £68,654.

It would appear to the student of political economy that these figures are out of proportion to the resources of the place; but it must be so, if every man who takes a medical degree feels it a hereditary right to enter the Government service. With rigid sanitation, carried out with an iron hand, backed up by the law, there is no reason why much economy could not be shown in this branch of the service, which for two colonies amounts to £145,534.

These lieutenant-governors would also occupy the position of sub-commandants-in-chief of the local military organizations, of which the governor-general would be commander-in-chief. Together with this office they would act as presidents over the local legislature, aided and advised by a competent staff, who would have no vote in the local Council.

The president would have power to veto all resolutions and local laws which conflict in any way with the constitution.

All matters vetoed by him as president of the local legislature must, if the exponent feels aggrieved, be taken to the federal assembly, to be threshed out there.

In this way a proper check would be kept on the local legislatures whose only redress would be to take their troubles to the federal assembly.

Such legislatures would be purely elective. The various colonies, after being divided up into electoral districts, would each elect their members to the local assembly, from which body men would be elected to the federal assembly without having to appeal to the population by another general election.

The present iniquitous system of refusing to vote a salary to our council-men so that their positions might be self-supporting, and in order to put an end to the popular belief that only men of means, even if they are without brains, can hope to gain admission to this august body, would be abolished.

Every council-man so elected for the local legislature would receive 10s. per day for every day he is in attendance on the Legislative Council, with travelling expenses.

Every member chosen for the General Assembly would receive 20s., with travelling expenses and free transportation by water or rail from their respective colonies to the seat of Government, the cruisers of the Confederacy being used as a means of quick transportation as much as is possible.

Members of the parochial board would receive 4s. per day, with mileage and other expenses.

Some argue that such methods would bring about a prostitution of the elective system, and prove a means of injecting undesirables into what is now an *exclusive circle*.

I, for my part, feel that it would promote and improve our elective system, even at the present day, and would be one of the surest means of bringing before the public men of ability, who would otherwise have been forced to remain obscure, from the fact that, being poor, and the institution not being a self-supporting one, he is consequently out of the race.

Wealth or position should not be the passport to our law-making bodies, for though wealth is a *gain*, it has its good and bad sides.

It is good when no regrets or remorse of conscience are associated therewith : it is bad when its accumulation is associated with regrettable events.

Socrates, in his Apology to the Dikastes, condemns the accumulation of wealth in the place of wisdom. He said: " You, a citizen of great and intelligent Athens, are not you ashamed to busy yourself to procure wealth, reputation, and glory in the greatest possible quantity—while you take neither thought nor pains about truth, or wisdom or fullest measure of goodness for your minds?"

What the greatest teacher of ancient and modern times tried to instil in the minds of his hearers was that *wisdom* was a far greater asset than *wealth*, and that a man's standing should be based upon the former quality instead of the latter.

The proof of his assertion is a living monument unto this day, for the rich man has left nothing of his wealth behind for coming generations, while the teachings of Socrates (*wisdom*) live on from generation to generation.

Nor is it to be imagined that the paying of our Legislature would be the means of inviting corruption into what some would condemn upon those very grounds as an unwholesome elective system, as far as the West Indies are concerned. Far from this! We should not anticipate an unlikely evil.

Every one knows that it is absolutely impossible to guard against all the various forms of corruption devised by men, high and low, some of which have crept into every system of election the world has known; but even in our wildest dreams we could never hope to approach the wholesale corruption which is perpetrated in elections in the mother country, which beat anything ever seen in the United States, the home of grafters.

The recent action of the English Courts, in unseating and declaring void the election of a member of the British Parliament, on the grounds of corruption in his election, is a most striking example, a parallel for which is seldom seen anywhere..

We need not hope to approach anything of the magnitude of the wholesale corruption which was carried on on behalf of this man by his election agents—from such we are safe.

The payment of our Legislatures would not, as some suppose, work a detriment to the colonies, or demoralize our politics. This scheme is not a new one by any means; it is done in the United States, Canada, and in most of the self-governing countries in the world. They, however, do not achieve this end through special taxation, but by paying their officials equitable and just salaries for their service, by refusing to pay pensions to any but those who are called upon, or are liable, to imperil their lives in defence of their native land, thereby leaving a comfortable margin to satisfy those who must devote their energies to the making of laws for the proper guidance of their country.

If it is possible to bring our minds to realize that the executive department of the Federal Government of the Dominion of Canada cost only £56,000, whilst that of the combined West Indian colonies cost not less than £124,000, a difference of £68,000, there is every reason to believe that, with economical treatment, we should in a short time find, on the credit side of our balance sheet, a fund sufficient to carry out our naval programme and defray all other current expenses.

Why is it that these colonies, with a total revenue of but £3,000,000, must be called upon to pay more than twice as much to their executive departments as the Dominion of Canada, whose present revenue is £20,000,000 ?

The great extravagance carried on in the West Indies, by the paying of exorbitant salaries on the one hand, and waste, through incompetency and indifference, on the other hand, is one of those matters which can only find its solution in the Colonial Office at Downing Street.

This is most striking when we recall the fact that the interests of the colonies have been on more than one occasion ruthlessly sacrificed by the Colonial Office, acting under the guidance of its advisers. We blame the secretary of this department only in so much as he allows himself to be led astray and misguided (being without personal knowledge) by those who have their own axes to grind.

This was decidedly so in the case of the coolie immigration to Trinidad, where the Premier, related by marriage to England's Prime Minister, was concerned on one hand, and the West Indian Committee and the rest of their *slave-holding friends* on the other.

We have not very far to go to find many other instances of neglect of the colonies' interest by this august department—the Colonial Office—one of which is the investment of the colonies' funds abroad in unprofitable bonds at a high rate of interest, with the principal showing a yearly decrease, to the colonies' loss, while our Public Works Departments are at the same time forced to raise loans abroad, at a higher rate of interest than that which we receive for our foreign investments.

Upon the instructions of its advisers the Colonial Secretary gave it out that investments of Government funds were unsafe in the West Indies; consequently our moneys went abroad to furnish labour to foreigners, while we famish for want of employment in order to gain that with which to procure the necessaries of life.

The interest paid on funds from the colonies invested abroad is from 3 to $3\frac{1}{2}$ per cent.—not more—but when we go a-borrowing we must pay $4\frac{1}{2}$ and 5 per cent. on all loans, which are of course floated in London. Although we have money to invest abroad, yet our public works are starved for the want of funds to see them through. Now, instead of having the English financiers risking their money and our paying a higher rate of interest for their loans than we receive on ours, why not let us assume our own risk, if we must take risks at all, to our own interest, and at a less rate? It is our money which is lost at home, yet this is not a hopeless loss, as from every loss some one gains.

Moreover, upon a change of mind from the Colonial Office, some funds were permitted latterly to be invested in the colonies, all of which have maintained their par, while those invested in Nigeria and the Straits Settlements have shown much depreciation.

If we are able to borrow at all, then let it be from our own funds as much as possible, at the same rate per cent. which we receive on our investments in foreign countries, and thus save ourselves $1\frac{1}{2}$ or 2 per cent. on the deal.

This would be a course which should surely tend to the uplift of those colonies which have any surplus to lend ; but the object of the Downing Street folk appears to be pointing in quite another direction.

We must be the feeding-ground, the producers, not the refiners—that is Britain's policy towards her West Indian colonies.

The following answer given by Colonel Seely, Under-Secretary of State for the Colonies, in June 1910, to a question put by Mr. Pointer— Labour member—in the House of Commons, on behalf of the people's association of British Guiana, goes far in explaining the cause of the backwardness of His Majesty's West Indian colonies :—

Q. Mr. Pointer : "Whether the *Colonial Office* was considering a railway scheme to run into the interior and gold regions of British Guiana."

A. Col. Seely : "No definite and acceptable scheme has yet been laid before the Colonial Office. Certain preliminary proposals were submitted to the Government by *a gentleman interested in the development of the colony,* but no definite offer had resulted."

According to the Under-Secretary the development of an important colony like British Guiana was not being pushed by the department under which it is run, but by " a gentleman interested in the development of the colony."

Is there, in the face of this answer, any mystery why we have not advanced abreast of the times ?

The total expenditure of the Commonwealth of Australia for the year 1908 was £6,513,000, while the aggregate expenditure for the British West Indian colonies (excluding Bermuda) for the same period was £3,175,000, which is nearly half as much.

Yet the revenue of the Commonwealth was £15,000,000, against the figures already quoted for the British West Indian possessions—which is not more than one-fifth.

The Lieutenant-Governors of Ontario and Quebec—either of which provinces is productive of more wealth than the combined West Indian colonies—receive but £2,000 annually as their salary, and they are the highest paid governors in the Dominion, while those of Jamaica and Trinidad receive £5,000 each, together with other luxuries.

It cannot be any longer reasoned that Europeans risk their health by residing in the tropics.

This might have been so a century or more ago, but to-day these tropical islands are, by improved sanitary methods, practically summer and winter resorts, where Europeans and Americans alike come to recoup their shattered health.

By what process, therefore, do those who are in authority justify the enormous salaries which are being paid to our European officials ? I am also willing to admit that they are not the only ones who are too highly paid for their services ; there are many others in every branch of the colonial service, and these are conspicuously noticeable in the customs department of Jamaica and Trinidad.

The scheme as laid out for responsible government for these colonies would give us a Federal Parliament, consisting of an Upper and Lower House and a House of Representatives for each of the colonial divisions—A, B, C, D, E, F, G, and H.

There would be a governor-general, aided by a privy council without a vote in parliament, eight lieutenant-governors, appointed by the governor-general upon the advice of the privy council, subject to the approval of the Federal Parliament for the eight divisions, namely : Barbados, Jamaica, Trinidad, and their dependencies, British Guiana, British Honduras, the Windward Islands, the Leeward Islands, and the Bahamas.

One of the so-called barriers, long entertained, against any proposition as to the federation of the West Indies, and which is continually harped upon by the anti-Federalists, is that of distance between the colonies.

This has, however, been rapidly minimized since the advent of fast transportation, and is no longer so formidable a foe to the project of the United West Indies as was formerly entertained.

I have only to point to the intercolonial sports, which are being carried out annually in the various West Indian possessions ; and the facility with which the men from the different colonies meet and fraternize shows that the bugbear " distance " is no longer to be feared.

Under self-government, fast and direct intercolonial steamers would be maintained and run by the union government, until some reliable private firm could be found to undertake to carry out this detail.

The periodical conflicts arising out of subsidies now paid to various steamship companies would be readily settled by initiating a line of steamers between these colonies and the mother country.

Steamships and other vessels bound for the United States, or on their way through the Panama Canal, and vice versa, would drop cargoes destined for distribution among the various West Indian colonies at the port most direct in their route, to be transhipped and carried to their final destination by our intercolonial boats.

Such a course would undoubtedly prove economical, both to the steamship companies and to importers.

The probable bone of contention that would appear on the scene along with Confederation of the West Indies, with responsible government, would be the choice of location of the chief seat of government—the Federal Parliament.

The Island of Jamaica, from its important position, being actually at the mouth of the Panama Canal, and its nearness to the United States of America, our largest customer, with a land-locked harbour, would without doubt claim serious attention.

Barbados, with its ancient rights, and central location being almost directly in the path of commerce, would come in for its share of consideration, while Trinidad, with its many rich and profitable industries, and tapping as it does the main artery of Venezuela's industry, though somewhat out of the way, would play a most prominent part in the bid for head-quarters.

I have ventured, seemingly, somewhat out of my latitude to touch the fringe of the garment of the government, which in my opinion would be best suited for these West Indian possessions under the new regime, and I trust that my readers will supply the missing links to complete the chain which I have attempted to forge.

CHAPTER XXII

THE POPULATION

To begin with, if we are to be prosperous and contented, as a federated people, we must find labour at home for our drifting population.

This is the only means by which we may hope to curtail the present wholesale exodus of our people to foreign lands in search of that which must support their families and pay their rates to the Government.

Surely such an acknowledged state of affairs for a British possession is, to say the least of it, shameful.

Surrounded by ill-governed countries, such as Venezuela, Colombia, and the Central American States, one would naturally expect to find the inhabitants of these admittedly badly governed countries flocking to those countries or colonies, which make it their boast to be able to show the rest of the world the way to success.

But we are pained to find things quite the reverse ; it is poverty, not prosperity, that follows in the wake of the British flag.

Instead of these people migrating to our shores in search of a livelihood, we find that it is the so-called better-governed people who are forced, from dire necessity, to rush to their shores in order to obtain that which is necessary to keep soul and body together. The following is taken from *The Standard*, a Barbados paper, dated June 1910, under the title of " Necessary Relief " :—

" The exodus from this island of persons of the lower middle class to the United States of America is greater this summer than in previous years.

" We are so accustomed to such immigration that we fail to notice its significance, but visitors to the island are fascinated by the stream of ambitious people, of all ages, who gaily leave the ' ever British Isle ' to seek dollars in the home of the bustling Yankees.

" On the whole these people do well abroad, and it must be said with satisfaction—they seldom fail to remember their poor relatives in the homeland, but are open-handed in relieving their pecuniary wants."

This is indeed a very frank admission of the stagnant state of affairs in this island.

The present form of government has had a fair trial ; it has been in existence in some of these colonies for centuries, and has proved a failure.

Give us a new one for this ancient and anti-quated form, which drains away the life-blood and saps the vitality.

Could Britain cry "Ungrateful!" if these colonies, in a body, were to strike out for annexation to the United States ? Patience is a virtue—and a great one, too, but surely it is not inexhaustible, more especially so when it is confronted with starvation and all the other miseries incident to an indifferent administration.

The situation needs a prompt remedy, for this state of affairs, despite our untiring and whole-souled loyalty, cannot be endured very much longer without revolt of some sort.

We must, if we are to hope for reasonable success under confederation, endeavour by every legitimate means to raise the standard of wages, and living generally, among the labouring classes.

There should be special legislation fixing the minimum wage for the labourer as well as his hours of labour.

In the British West Indian colonies, under the present system of government, there still exists the old custom of hoarding lands in accordance with the English landlord system.

Land is the keynote of all the requirements which man seeks on earth—it is the wealth of nations and the foundation of commerce.

I repeat—to be prosperous and contented there must be the land to cultivate, backed up by the scientific knowledge how to do so properly, in order that satisfactory and beneficial results may be derived therefrom.

Why should one man be allowed to stow away hundreds of acres of land, while there are others who, for the want of land to cultivate, are forced to migrate to foreign countries, there to make their homes—forced by circumstances—while the Government stands apparently impotent to do the first thing to remedy this great evil ?

The absence of the middle-man in our law-making bodies is chiefly responsible for the present backward condition of these colonies, and so long as the present system obtains, so long will the interest of His Majesty's subjects in these islands be devoid of that fostering care which alone can procure and maintain prosperity and satisfaction.

In small communities such as we are able to boast of, this system of *hoarding land* for speculative and other purposes should not be tolerated for one moment.

This is no new theory that I am expounding. Members of our several legislative bodies know this fact, but cannot act contrary to it ; for to do so would be detrimental to their own interest.

Under federation, with self-government, it might occur to the administration to acquire by purchase, at a fixed rate, all lands over and above those actually under cultivation or pasturage.

All lands so acquired in conjunction with other government lands would be apportioned in homestead lots, of from twenty-five to fifty acres, to those peasants who are in need of land to cultivate, under the " Occupation and Purchase Rights " system, similar to that now in operation in New Zealand.

The system is as follows :—If a man takes up fifty acres of land under the system, at the price of £1 per acre, his total indebtedness to the Government would be £50, to be paid within a given time.

He is required to pay an interest of from 3 to 5 per cent. on the total value of his indebtedness to the Government annually, as rental during his period of occupation.

During the first year he is required to put in 15 per cent. of improvement, under governmental supervision, and the same for the second, third, and fourth years.

At the end of the fifth year he is required to construct a house and reside on the land.

At the end of the seventh year he is required to put in improvements amounting to the value of his entire holding.

At the end of the twenty-fifth year, or at any period between the seventh and the twenty-fifth (year) he may purchase the freehold outright and receive a governmental title for same.

This plan makes the burden of payment as light as possible for the occupant, and insures at the same time the cultivation of the land upon scientific and economical principles.

To facilitate such a scheme under federation, in the West Indies, there would be established bureaus of seeds, soil, and plants, at the expense of the Federal Government.

Seeds and plants would be freely distributed to the planters, under such regulations as would prevent the favourites, who are found in almost every body, from ousting other deserving applicants.

By this method it would be hoped to regenerate and carry on successfully, the backbone of all industries—agriculture—from the position to which it has been relegated, to a point where it would be found interesting and more profitable, in these colonies, than had hitherto been experienced.

Better equipped school gardens than those now established in some of the West Indian colonies would be established throughout the Federation in connection with elementary schools.

Following this procedure we should strive to make an agricultural people out of those who are now wringing their hands and asking, What is to be done ? While the soil is calling aloud for tillers.

The present method of cultivating lands in the West Indies, for most of the minor products, among the small settlers, is to cut down five or ten acres of land for one year's crop, and then move on each succeeding year to another " five " or " ten " acres ; and in this way within ten years not less than fifty or a hundred acres of fertile land is run over and abandoned as impoverished and deemed to be unfit for further tilling, when in reality the soil had been barely touched.

In Great Britain and Ireland, and in many European countries, many generations have been known to be reared up on a simple plot of land of from five to ten acres, out of which they gain all the necessary support, from time to time, besides being able to lay aside a substantial sinking fund,

This is, however, not the question of the moment. The issue which I have endeavoured to make paramount in this book is—Confederation of the British West Indian colonies, with colonial self-government. This is the music (figuratively speaking) that I have been attempting to play for the benefit of my readers.

Will it appeal to their sympathies and self-respect as freemen ? Shall I be condemned or applauded for the presentation of this new proposition ? The future alone will be able to tell the verdict.

I have already dealt somewhat at length on the chief aim of this book, and now I propose to say that the next item, a new and additional feature of importance, is " Colonial Preference."

Yes ! preference from the mother country on the products from the West Indies going into British markets, which is likely to bring less trouble, if any, than the proposed preference on Canadian goods coming into the West Indies.

The United Empire would fall short of its purpose, if trade within the Empire was not signalized by preference from the mother country.

Passing on to the scheme in aid of Imperial defence in conjunction with our federation, the question of an army in the shape of a National police force, conjoined with a militia, well-drilled and equipped, and backed up by compulsory military education ; also a navy equipped and manned for the most part by the Federated Colonies, has been gone into—but to maintain an

army and navy there must be the population to
draw upon.

In this respect we are sadly wanting. Will
sanitation, the preventive medicine of the age,
do the *trick* in time to come ? This is one of our
hopes.

Would the proposed new regime (government
by the people for the people) draw English immigrants and the millions of intelligent American
negroes to our shores ?

With the exception of the importation of slaves
from Africa centuries ago, the question of immigration to the West Indies seems never to have
been taken seriously into consideration.

The matter, however, appears somewhat doubtful of success, since the attempt to entice English
immigrants to Australia and Canada, where
climatic conditions are somewhat similar to those
existing in their own land, has been an uphill
game.

The conclusion, therefore, is that where these
countries have failed the West Indies need not
hope for success. I say this is not so.

If we have anything to offer, our hopes under
new conditions bid fair to soar higher than those
of the Commonwealth or the Dominion.

Already there is a gleam of hope in the mam-
moth scheme of Lord Mountstephen, who has
recently established a fund of £60,000 for the
promotion of immigration and establishment in
the colonies of *waifs* of the slums of London.

It is to be hoped that others will follow his lead

and that the scheme will embrace the " United " West Indies.

We can no longer look to Africa for additional supplies; the East Indian, I feel, would not be looked upon as undesirable if he came at his own expense and as a settler; but India is far away, and only men of means can afford to travel the distance.

It can be unhesitatingly said in defence of the opposition to coolie immigration for " specific time and purpose " that their presence in our midst under such conditions is a blot upon British civilization, and a detriment to our native labouring population.

Their wants are fewer than the clothes-wearing natives, they accept a lower scale of wages from individuals and combinations, who can well afford to pay labour its value.

This they do in direct opposition to our native labourer, whom they thus outstrip, because the man with the larger necessities to satisfy cannot compete with this lowered scale.

The average East Indian will tell you how many thousand dollars he has accumulated by this method and sent to Calcutta, but still he refuses to substitute the garb of civilization for his semi-nude and disgraceful condition.

Sir Daniel Morris has recorded to the effect "that the importation of coolie labour does not affect the wages of the negro labourer, and that the negroes of the West Indies are hereditarily disinclined to continuous work."

I say, in direct contradiction to that assertion, that this is not so, and that Sir Daniel has gathered a very erroneous impression.

Who cleaned the streets of Trinidad before the coolies came ? The natives, of course. Who cleans them now ? The coolies—and why ? Because they can be employed for a pittance, in so much that even the Public Works Department is ready to avail itself of this cheap labour to the disadvantage of the native labourer—the taxpayer.

The presence of these immigrants in the West Indies, under the present conditions, is nothing less than the fight of capital against labour, except that in our case the aid, voice, and funds of the Government are brought to bear, in order to coerce the ratepayer into submission : and why is this possible ?

I say the root is deeply buried in our present system of government.

Their presence in our midst is ascribed to the weakened state of our cane industry necessitating the importation of what looks, at first sight, like cheap labour, as a sort of government subsidy, at an enormous cost to the colonies.

If the cultivation of this product cannot yield sufficient to pay its way and also show a substantial profit, then it is evident that this industry cannot stand on its own legs and ought to be dropped as a losing concern.

There is no justifiable reason for artificially sustaining its life at such a great sacrifice of human freedom and treasure, in the interest of a *chosen few.*

Are we to continue to feel that we are, at our own loss, intended to satisfy British manufacturers, and to furnish labour to the British working-man ?

This seems hardly possible ; yet, under existing conditions, this is the only feasible inference that can be drawn.

Wouldn't it be much better to spend the moneys now used in importing these coolies, the upkeep of an immigration bureau, the cost of maintenance in hospitals and prisons, in subsidizing the cane-farmers, and in stimulating peasant proprietary ?

Why should the West Indies import labourers from distant India, when Barbados, Jamaica, and Trinidad have sufficient to put through the Panama Canal and enough to spare ?

There seems to lie at the bottom of it all, deeply imbedded, the inherent desire on the part of some to carry on a slow system of slavery, and which is only possible with *coolie labour,* since the native West Indian will resent being kicked and cuffed about, as most coolies will permit.

It is a direct mandate from capital to labour which reads, Take the humble shilling that you are offered, or I will take your own stick and break your head (by bringing in coolie labourers with your own money, who will gladly accept less), and thus starve you and your family into submission or out of existence.

This has been the undoing of the labour conditions in the West Indies. It was this very method of treating the labouring man, to a great extent, in England, that led to the Wat Tyler rebellion, soon after the ravages caused by the Black Death, when the labourers' statute was enacted to coerce the labourer into accepting a regular rate of wages, which was not commensurate with the scale of living.

We earnestly hope that no similar consequence will arise in the West Indies as a result of unjust labour competition ; but surely the condition is becoming desperate and calls for immediate remedial measures.

One of the pleas in justification of the importation of coolie labour to these colonies, at the taxpayers' expense, is that the negro (or native labouring class) is inherently indisposed to work more than five days in a week, and as the cane industry needs a class of constant labour, the necessity for the introduction of the East Indian coolie labour is thereby created.

In the first place, the coolie comes under contract, which binds him to work for a certain number of days in a week. One of three places he must occupy—the field, the jail, or the hospital—and this accounts for his much-bolstered-up reputation as a constant labourer.

His working capacity is the natural outcome of his indenture, which is incident to every class of contract labour, examples of which have had ample demonstration on the works of the Panama Canal.

When we take into consideration that the time-expired coolie promptly loses his reputation gained on the estate, to work six days in a week, and does little or no work thereafter which entails any serious amount of manual labour, it is easy to see that his accredited working qualities are not voluntary but forced ones, incident to the conditions contained in his contract.

It is no secret that the average coolie, of the class we get as labourers, is a very lazy mortal, in so much that for the want of planting sufficient rice in India to support his family, thousands of them die yearly of starvation, and the Government is helpless, from the fact that at home or abroad they will not lead and must be driven.

This is not such an easy task in turbulent and seditious India as it is on the estates in the colonies.

The following is culled from the *Madras Weekly Mail* :—

" There is no doubt that the old order of things is changing in India to such an extent that, if the natives do not manage to secure *higher wages* or much larger supplies of food stuff (by means of improved systems of cultivation, manuring, and irrigation), famine and food riots from sheer desperation, far worse than the present political disturbances, may occur."

Quite contrary to the official reputation which this coolie labour has on record at Downing Street, we find that, in the West Indies, he is not only opposed to continuous labour, but he dislikes labour on the cane estates.

There can be no greater burden imaginable, and of such a distasteful nature to the majority of ratepayers, than that of the annual expenditure upon this class of labour, which is worthless and productive of no material benefit to these colonies.

According to Dr. G. H. Mason's paper, read before the Agricultural Society of Trinidad, B.W.I., entitled " Indentured Labour and Preventive Disease," dated June 22, 1910 :

"There were ten thousand indentured coolies distributed among the various estates of that colony.

" The entries on the books of the several estates showed that 28,592 cases of disease were admitted for treatment in the public hospital annually, or, roughly speaking, *three* hospital entries for each coolie, where he lays up for an average of nine days."

This does not, however, include the days when they are sick enough to rest up, and not sufficiently ill to be sent to the hospital.

On these occasions it is common talk that they are forced to go out to their tasks, and if they refuse they are promptly taken before the magistrates and sent to jail for failing to keep to the terms of their contract.

These " slaves " are not permitted to leave the estate without a pass duly signed, the granting of which is not prescribed by law, but is entirely at the option of the overseer.

Any privileged officer on the property, or of the

police force, can stop any coolie found beyond the precincts of the plantation, interrogate him, and examine his pass.

If he has the necessary " strip," then he may go free, but without this he goes to jail in the customary railroad fashion.

The following correctly illustrates the manner in which coolie labourers are dealt with in these colonies :—

" TRINIDAD, COUVA POLICE COURT, *July* 12, 1910.—*Desertion.*—Mr. J. Knox, of Waterloo Estate, charged Bajnath, an indentured immigrant, with desertion since May 20, 1910. The defendant, who was previously convicted for this offence, pleaded guilty and was sentenced to thirty days' hard labour."

This example is what can be justly termed an almost daily occurrence.

" July 15, 1910.—SAN FERNANDO, Mr. ——, an overseer on the Bien Venue Estate, the property of Tennants Estates, Ltd., on being attacked by some indentured immigrants, shot two of his assailants in self-defence.

" One man, shot through the lung, died soon after ; the other, shot in the groin, is lying in a precarious condition at the San Fernando Hospital.

" Mr. —— was arrested, charged with manslaughter for killing one ——, an 'indentured immigrant.'

" He was remanded on bail at £200. It

appears that on Thursday, some immigrants refused to work, and the *overseer* reported *five* of them, as they were the ringleaders.

" The men got wind of the fact that legal proceedings were being taken against them. Knowing what the result would be they got in an ugly mood, attacked the *overseer* (with sticks), and the result was that a coolie was killed and another wounded.

" Mr. ———'s plea was that he acted in self-defence, and he produced evidence to support his statement. He was acquitted before the examining magistrate."

This unfortunate occurrence is the direct result of a system which, so far as my knowledge goes, appertains only to convict gangs and slavery; still these men are called free men and British subjects at that.

I maintain that every form of contract labour which deprives an individual of his personal liberty and freedom is slavery ; and every one who becomes a party to such contracts is engaged in the traffic of slaves.

Dr. Mason further explains " That the cost of maintaining 28,592 cases (sick coolies) in the public hospital for nine days at fifteen cents per day (the very lowest rates) is something well over £8,000.

There is also the prison maintenance for which no figures are available, the cost of repatriation and the upkeep of immigration bureaus at the annual cost of £9,000—which is £7,000 more than it costs the Dominion of Canada to run her Indian Department.

The most interesting part of the accounting is the importation of these coolies : in the year 1907–8 the Island of Trinidad paid for the introduction of 1,860 of these immigrants (at £27 per head) a sum in excess of £50,000 for this system of modern slavery.

This amount was increased by £9,000 for the batch that was brought over the following year, but the total cost to the taxpayers for the presence of this large population of East Indians in the colonies is correctly estimated at £6,000,000 paid through a number of years.

Is this cheap labour ? In the Immigration Committee's report the following comparative figures are given :—In 1829 the sugar exported was 22,361 tons, and in 1910 it was about 45,000 (tons).

Dealing with the Island of Trinidad the Committee found that " in 1829, before the introduction of coolie labour, the production of sugar was 22,361 tons."

Subsequent to that, in the year 1845, after various experiments were tried to introduce labourers from the neighbouring island, from the Kroo Coast and Madeira, but failed to materialize, the first batch of imported immigrants (coolies) numbering 237.

Sixty-five years after (1845–1910) the production of sugar was 45,000 tons, says the committee, an increase of 22,639 tons (an average of about 302 tons, slightly more or less, annually) over and above what it was in the year 1829.

During the same period 116,715 coolies were brought into the colony at the cost of £3,150,496, an average annual cost of £42,000 more or less, against the average annual production (increase) of 301 tons of sugar valued at £14 per ton, or £4,214, which shows a loss, according to the yearly average, of over £37,000.

I have already stated that the increase on the output since 1827 is 22,639 tons, which were the figures before the commission in 1908.

It took 10,000 coolies to produce this gain, with the aid of native negro labourers, and which was marketed at £316,946. From this amount the sum of £60,726 must be deducted on behalf of the part played by the cane-farmers, leaving the amount of £256,220.

The cost of the introduction of the (10,000) coolies to produce this increase is estimated at £270,000, or £27 for each coolie, to which must be added £8,000 for hospital attendance (less the expense upon the judicature and prisons), making a total of £278,000, against £256,220, as the income on sugar production, which shows a deficit of £21,780 against sugar production for the year 1908.

Yet these figures do not show the full extent of the deficit, for it must be remembered that native labour plays an important part in the harvesting of the sugar crop (the coolies for the most part not being strong enough for the work), which reduces to a great extent the output claimed for these immigrants.

The cane-farmers during the same year contributed 139,000 tons of cane, which were grown on lands allotted to them on sixteen estates, which went into the total crop of 380,000 tons of cane grown by the estates.

It appears from these figures that cane-farming ought to be stimulated by an annual subsidy from the Government, as an encouragement along those lines.

If the Indian Government finds itself embarrassed by an overcrowded population, it should furnish those persons who desire to immigrate with the necessary passage, and sufficient means to start life as agriculturists outside India.

If there are some parties in the West Indies who have a decided weakness for coolie labourers, and prefer them to all others, they should be made to bear the *whole cost* of their introduction.

But one cannot conceive why the general public should be taxed to bring in immigrants from India, while maintaining an immigration fee to the exclusion of a freer intercourse among the several West Indian colonies from which labourers could be obtained.

It has been shown that the cost of introducing these coolies over a period of sixty-five years runs up to millions for a single colony.

Of this sum 21 per cent. is contributed by the planters, 52 per cent. on all estates (whether they use indentured labour or not), and 27 per cent. from the general revenue.

The first two items (21 and 52 per cent.) are chargeable to the produce output of the colony, with the consequent effect, that the sale of cocoa from estates which do not use indentured labour are directly hampered by this additional tax.

In the second place the taxpayers who do not use these immigrants, besides having to contribute 27 per cent. from the general revenue, must bear the increase on this article which is consumed locally, and must also contribute to their support in prisons and hospitals.

The committee on Indian immigration to Crown Colonies cannot be taken seriously when they put themselves on record to the effect that :

" These immigrants bring such prosperity to the colonies to which they are sent that it is not out of reason that the places receiving them should contribute to their coming in from the general revenue."

This is the " stock argument " of the Colonial Office and West Indian Committee, which carries weight only from the fact that the Government at Downing Street has the means of forcing it upon us.

But why fetch these people here ? Why not send them to desolate Australia at the expense of the Australians? No! That would be a dangerous experiment, too much so to be seriously entertained.

Yet from all that can be gathered, Australia's need of immigration is much greater than that of the West Indian colonies, but Australia is not a Crown colony and that's a big difference.

Unlike the self-governing countries, we are willing to admit all classes of immigrants, but it doesn't seem profitable to pay a premium on the system.

The same commission that reported on the immigration of coolies to the colonies decided that immigration is the best condition for the colonies. That is true; but Canada needs immigrants more than we do: why not send them there?

Are not these coolies more skilled in planting rice than cane?

It is a condition which helps India and the Indian, says the Indian Government, who would like to have the Indians with savings return home while a new batch is despatched on the fortune-hunting expedition.

As the report points out, the sending of the coolies to the colonies is not primarily for the development of the colonies, but for the betterment of the Indians themselves.

That " the system is not open to *serious* objection " is sufficient admission, on the part of the commissioners, that it is open to *some form of objection,* which might not to them seem serious ; and I take it that that is the one form to which we have always held : viz., that the colonies should not be made to contribute to the presence of the coolies here.

I desire to make it plain that we are not opposed to immigration, be they East Indian coolies, Africans, or Europeans; but what we seriously object to is the matter of being compelled to pay for their introduction and maintenance.

It must be borne in mind that, while there is considerable opposition against the method employed in bringing coolie immigrants here at the taxpayers' expense, the feeling is not totally against him as a man immigrating for the betterment of his condition.

Indeed, the offspring of these coolies, born in the colonies, have become very useful members of society, where they exert an influence for good among their own people, and will be a factor to be reckoned with by the governing head as soon as they shall have attained sufficient numerical strength

We want immigrants, hence we cannot be opposed to immigration as a scheme: what we say and maintain is that the present system is both unwholesome and undesirable, and ought to be dispensed with, in the face of our professing civilization and freedom.

If Britain loses these colonies, it will be on account of the use of the *mailed fist* in one direc-

tion, and her indifference to the wishes of the
people ; for no people, no matter how loyal they
may be, will long submit to this one-man policy
in these enlightened times, with the weapon of
" cessation " so close at hand.

CHAPTER XXIII

THE DREAD OF THE WHITE CIRCLE

I HAVE already dealt with the subject of race animosity between the negroes and the whites of the British West Indian possessions, wherein it is shown that " we have no race problem of any moment to solve."

It has, however, been long hinted by the more pessimistic minds that the white population of the West Indies, who, by the way, form a very small but influential part of the community, would oppose any plan for extensive political freedom of these colonies, for fear of negro domination.

To the reader who has been brought up under " responsible government " the first thing that would occur to his mind would be, How can a possible objection from the smaller portion of the inhabitants block any progressive move for self-government ?

He has only to look up the past and present history of British Crown Colony Government to learn that here is where the minority rules.

This section unjustly fear that liberal political freedom would lead to uprisings against them on the part of the negro population ; but this much-dreaded outlook is more imaginary than real and cannot be borne out by facts based on the present relationship of the two peoples.

By reason of the same fear they would much prefer to see these possessions pass from one mastery to another—the Americans preferred—rather than see the negro taking a substantial part in the government of their native land.

Experience will bear me out that there is no fear of negro uprising in the West Indies of any magnitude, if at all.

Disturbances of this nature in the past have had white men as the chief disturbing factors, who, using the ignorant negroes as their tool, encouraged them to oppose organized law and order ; but this is no longer possible.

This was so in the case of the " water riot " in Trinidad, which culminated in a terrible disaster for the rioters.

As in other silly uprisings and the still more silly method of suppressing them, in British Crown Colonies, modern rifles of the military were brought into play against the sticks and stones of these disturbers of the peace, and many were mercilessly, and it is alleged indiscriminately, shot down by the men under arms.

This method of suppression was excessive and without comparison—alas ! " Spain can no longer boast pre-eminence in barbarity," in the presence of such atrocities.

The parties who had the grievance (the whites) did their part by displaying fire-arms in conspicuous places where a mob could easily procure them : they made violent and riotous speeches, inciting the populace (the negroes) to act, but beyond this they took no part in the squabble.

Hence it was that the news was soon flashed abroad that the negroes of Trinidad were up in arms : had taken to the hills and were burning down the city of Port of Spain. What a nightmare !

Thus he bears the stigma of being rebellious when in reality he had merely been the tool of the capitalists, the forces behind him, a condition which is not applicable to negroes alone, but to the masses of any country.

It would be quite unfair and a misfortune, if these misunderstandings, regardless of those responsible for them, should be taken as a blot on the West Indies ; for what country, for that matter, that has not had its internal strife ?

Read the early history of the mother country and ponder over the chaotic state of her internal affairs during that period. Who would have thought that a people who lived only in mud-huts and worshipped the mistletoe, and who fought, bickered, and scratched among themselves at every possible moment like " Kilkenny cats," were destined to become the rulers of the world ?

Is there then no hope for the negro, who at present enjoys far better advantages than did the early Britons ?

The urgent need of the British West Indian

possessions is not the driving out, or a depopulation, of its white inhabitants, but the solution of a means of encouraging their further immigration to these colonies.

The white, black, and coloured people throughout the West Indies are on the very best of terms : they understand each other socially, politically, and otherwise, and there is every indication that this brotherly spirit of loving and trusting one another will continue indefinitely.

There has never been found the necessity of enacting special legislation to keep the two races apart or together, and there never will be so long as we steer clear of Yankee mastery.   Every one exercises absolute freedom of will : thus far we are blessed.

Experience has amply demonstrated that all that the negroes of the West Indies seek is an opportunity to exist, as becomes a people who, by virtue of their civilization and advancement, deserve some consideration : and if they were given this they would never seek to know the age of the moon.

Their miseries are tied up in their wants and oppressions, and not in the spirit of mastery or domination over the *whites* : and now we come to the

CONCLUSION

wherein the whole situation is summed up as follows :—*Confederation of the British West Indian Colonies, with responsible government, as the only means of checking ultimate annexation to the United States of America.*

Commercial relations with Canada so far as convenient and practicable, but not to the exclusion of the United States, or in such a way that might be construed as an affront by the great American nation—our commercial friend.

We do not wish for political affiliation with the Dominion, the Canadians do not desire it, and for us such a course would be equivalent to placing the last straw which broke the camel's back.

It is the earnest hope of the West Indies that in the near future Canada will find herself in a position to take the bulk of our produce, if necessary, and send us an equal quantity of food stuffs and other commodities in exchange.

But at the present juncture it does not seem that, with a population of five or six millions, she is capable of taking care of the entire surplus output of these colonies, which does not find its way into the English markets.

It will be observed that, throughout this volume, the appeal for federation, with responsible government, is made with the negro in the foreground.

This has been done, not from any selfish motive or disregard for the feelings of the white inhabitants of these possessions, but on the premise that the negro forms the bulk of the population of these colonies, and consequently should receive first consideration.

One of the principles underlying self-government is that the voice of the majority rules.

It may be that ere this book is put into circulation great changes may have taken place, in consequence of the rapid movement of events, for and against many of the ideas advocated or decried herein : however, be that as it may, time alone will prove whether or not the prognostications contained herein have been justified, in whole or in part, by subsequent events.

It is my hope that every West Indian who reads this book, be he white, black, or of mixed blood, will, after allowing for all discrepancies in its composition and other shortcomings, resolve within himself that : Here's another vote for this just and most equitable cause—The Confederation of the British West Indian Colonies, with Colonial self-government, as against their Annexation to the United States of America.

CHAPTER XXIV

THE COLONIES

GENERAL REMARKS

THE British West Indian possessions, conspicuous as examples of British autocracy, have many sides of interest.

If we admit that enough has been said on the subject of their maladministration it appears fitting that something should be said of the general characteristics of the most important of them.

One of the greatest drawbacks to these colonies is the amount of undeveloped land, held by private local syndicates and individuals, who do not reside in the tropics, which is allowed to lie waste, and last, but not least, by the Government under the title of Crown Lands.

During the year 1910 the tax levied on undeveloped land in Australia reached the respectable sum of *one million pounds sterling*.

It is said that the rates levied on such property are almost prohibitive, but this must in the end work out for the betterment of the country, as it will force the development of land which had hitherto been lying idle.

With regard to " union, " it will be seen that the linking of the Turk's and Caicos Islands with Jamaica, Tobago with Trinidad, and the joining together of the Leeward and Windward Islands, where the individual colony was too poor to support a high-salaried governor, show that there has been some feeble attempt at Federation by the folks in Downing Street.

A general confederation of the British possessions in the West Indies, though tending to furnish still fewer lucrative posts, would only be taking the matter a step farther, consistent with the general tide of affairs and with our advanced civilization.

Only then could we look forward to a *United West Indian Civil Service*, and representation in the parliament of the Empire.

But, try as I may, I find it utterly impossible to dissociate the problem of responsible government from any scheme of general federation for the West Indies.

I have already said that confederation is not a new thing to these colonies—indeed not.

As far back as 1764 there existed a partial federation of the British possessions in the West Indies, but this was confined only to the Windward Islands, and it prospered for a century or more.

The islands concerned were St. Vincent, Grenada, Dominica, Tobago, Barbados, and St. Lucia, with Barbados as headquarters.

In the light of the enlarged scheme for a general

federation of the Empire, we must endeavour to discard from our minds the idea of a separation of the commercial from the political union—this is impossible.

I cannot conceive the existence of the one without the other, so intimately connected is legislation with commerce.

We must not allow ourselves to be hoodwinked into a purely commercial unification, this would rather increase than decrease our present obligations.

There can be no beneficial union of these possessions short of political emancipation: the only question to be decided is whether absolute self-government should be compromised for a representative form.

It is plain that to unite these colonies under one head, with a centralized administration, they must either all be reduced to Crown colonies, or be elevated to responsible or representative government, owing to their present complex form of administration.

The former is not possible, as this would be a retrograde step, and a set-back to the plans for the United Empire of Great Britain; for in this great union not a speck of British territory should be excluded, or placed in a position of inferiority.

The only feasible conclusion, therefore, is that they must be elevated to the status of self-governing states, as a means to the accomplishment of this most necessary change—the Federation of the British Empire.

JAMAICA

THIS island, situated in the Caribbean Sea, within forty-eight hours of the Panama Canal and four days of the United States of America, is the largest of the British West Indian Islands.

It is 144 miles long, 50 miles wide, about 360 miles in circumference, and contains 4,207 square miles—about half the size of Wales.

Its total acreage is estimated at 2,692,480, of which 873,229 are under cultivation, 80,000 in swamps and inaccessible lands, and 1,739,171 still available for tilling.

The correct date of the discovery of Jamaica by Columbus appears to have been in 1494, on the morning of the 3rd day of May.

The island, a Spanish possession by right of discovery, remained in their hands for over a century and a half (160 years), when it was captured by the English under Admiral Penn and Venables, in 1655, acting under orders of Cromwell.

There remained, however, still some question as to the ownership of the island, and it was not until the year 1670, fifteen years after its surrender, when the Treaty of Madrid was concluded, that Britain's title to it was finally settled.

The population of Jamaica according to the last census is given at 840,000, or more, of which only 2 per cent. are " pure " white, the remaining portion for the most part being of African descent—three-fifths being pure-blooded negroes, with about 15,000 coolies.

Upon the accession of Charles II. to power he abolished the military regime left by the Cromwells, and granted the colonials a constitution in its stead, which existed for nearly two hundred years. This was a purely representative institution.

In 1865 a rebellion broke out among the black population, which is said to have been instigated by aggrieved members of the white community.

The insurrection was suppressed by Governor Eyre, then chief executive of the island, with the same unnecessary force (so characteristic of our colonial governors) that was exhibited by Governor Malony of Trinidad in the following century. Thus, in more than one instance, West Indian history repeats itself.

In 1866 the Constitution granted by Charles II. was surrendered for anything that His Majesty's Government might feel disposed to substitute in lieu thereof.

The reason assigned for this great sacrifice of freedom was that the depression caused by the abolition of slavery (the slave owners got over £6,000,000), coupled with the fact that the existing assembly refused to vote supplies, etc., was a sufficient cause for its surrender.

But the real gist of the situation seemed, however, to have been brought about by the presence of the negro as a *free man*, in a country with a representative institution, where he completely outnumbered his former masters.

This was evidently the great underlying cause, for we find soon after the suppression of the insurrection, which was confined only to a small section of the island (one parish), His Majesty's representative, Governor Eyre, at a meeting of the legislature urging the unsuitability of the existing form of government to meet the *changed conditions*.

The frightened legislature readily responded to his demands, and abrogated the existing form of government, which had served well for nigh two centuries.

In 1869 a new legislature, consisting of official and non-official members, was established. This regime, after existing for only fifteen years was (1884) amended to the present form.

Fully two centuries after the discovery of this island (1692), its first great earthquake recorded in history occurred.

Port Royal, the capital, and headquarters of the " buccaneers," was completely wiped out.

Since that date, with the exception of an occasional light shock, the people of the rebuilt town of Port Royal and the new commercial centre Kingston, which sprang into life soon after the destruction of the former, were never in imminent peril from earthquakes.

Another two centuries had rolled by peacefully without giving the slightest indication of an approaching catastrophe when, in 1907, the city of Kingston with its 49,000 souls was completely destroyed in broad daylight, by a most devastating earthquake, with great loss of life.

It was then that the historian's memory flashed back, with the rapidity which characterizes a flash of lightning, to 1692 and Port Royal.

Two hundred and two years after the colony's discovery it was visited by a calamitous earthquake. Two hundred and fifteen years after this visitation another misfortune, due to the same cause, with far-reaching effect, again fell upon its inhabitants. Will there be a repetition of these calamities during the twenty-first century ? Quien sabe ?

In Jamaica, as in the other British West Indian possessions, the education of the past, present, and future generations was never a question of any great moment to the Government.

The educational facilities in this and other West Indian colonies are chiefly denominational, and where helped by the Government (most of them are) they are called assisted schools.

Children, male and female, are forced to leave school at a tender age (fourteen years), and there being no free secondary or governmental provisions for a general free, secondary free, or technical education, the bulk of the inhabitants, being too poor to pay for private tuition, find themselves unfit, from an educational standpoint, to occupy any position of responsibility.

This lack of a *free secondary* education for boys and girls throughout the West Indies contributes, more than any other item, to the backwardness of the mass of British West Indian negroes.

Among the many products of the colony are to be found bananas, sugar, coffee, ginger, cocoa, cotton, spices, oranges, dyewood, coco-nuts, copper, (some) gold, etc.

Bananas as an item of export once reached the respectable mark of $1\frac{1}{4}$ million pounds sterling, of which the major portion went to the United States.

Now that the Yankees have proposed growing bananas in hothouses, if successful, the islanders will find their chief mainstay taxed and discriminated against, which will bring about a howl for annexation to the big " North American brother," in spite of every other visible and imaginary disadvantage.

The only political body in the island worthy of mention is the National Club, organized and presided over by the Hon. S. Gilbert Cox, barrister-at-law.

Its field of action has up to this been purely local, but every hope is entertained that it will soon see its way clear to partake of functions in accord with its name.

The " National Club " has put new vigour into the

political life of the island, and has been the means of rousing the bulk of the population out of its long slumber.

Steam communication between the colony and the outside world is carried on through the agency of several steamship lines, among which is the Royal Mail Steam Packet Co., long identified with the colony's "ups and downs," the Leyland, and Hamburg-American Line.

The existing form of government is Autocratic.

BRITISH HONDURAS

This colony is to be found on the Central American coast, bounded on the east by the Caribbean Sea, on the north by Mexican territory, and on the south by Guatemala.

Its total area is about 7,562 square miles, of which only 80 square miles are estimated as under cultivation.

As far back as 1630 the affairs of the colony were supervised by the government and council of Jamaica.

This continued for over two centuries, until 1884, when the colony was declared independent of Jamaica, thus providing room for an extra colonial governor.

The past history of British Honduras has not been altogether uneventful.

From a kingdom it has descended to the unenviable position of a British Crown colony.

Between the years 1839 and 1870 there existed in this colony a most liberal constitution, which, after existing for about thirty-two years, gave up the ghost, and the substitution of a new form of administration was left to the discretion of His Majesty's Government.

There is abundant room for stock-farming in British Honduras. Towards the west there is an immense prairie, capable of supporting an abundance of cattle, but little or no effort is being made to utilize on a large scale this natural feeding-ground.

Half the world's supply of beef can find an outlet through the English markets.

Most of the cattle slaughtered annually in Liverpool comes from abroad, Venezuela, Texas (U.S.A.), etc., but not a horn from the British West Indian colonies.

Britain in time of war must depend mainly on the friendliness of the United States for its mounts and meat supplies. Why so, when we have so much room in these colonies for the rearing of cattle, horses, and mules, for " our " Army ?

Will not the Imperial Government come to the rescue ? If not, will not the local government rescue itself ?

Should some one ask, What can the Government do ? I venture to suggest : Let us imagine that the Government buys 10,000 head of cattle and divides them into 40 lots of 250 each.

The next thing, a lottery is put up, with forty winning numbers, and the cattle-rearing inhabitants of that particular colony are invited to participate—having previously supplied evidence to the Government of their individual ability to care for a given number.

The winners thereby become debtors to the Government, to the extent of the value of their winnings.

They are then allowed twenty or thirty years to pay for the lots, while they, in the meantime, pay an annual interest of from 2 to 5 per cent. until their total indebtedness is liquidated by a system of instalments.

Such a course would seem to be somewhat more satisfactory than the investments which we now make in *foreign securities*, which never show any substantial gain.

The main industry of British Honduras is to be found

in its choice woods : viz. :—mahogany and cedar ; also
some bananas and coco-nuts.

In 1907 about 10,000,000 feet of mahogany were exported. At about the same period, 4½ million coco-nuts
and a million bunches of bananas were also exported,
for the most part to the United States.

Government—Autocratic.

TRINIDAD

The colony of Trinidad is among the most important
of British West Indian possessions and is to be found in
the southern part of the Caribbean Sea.

It is separated from the coast of Venezuela by the
Gulf of Paria and a narrow passage about 7½ miles
wide, called the " Bocas " or Dragon's Mouth.

The island is about 55 miles long, 40 miles broad at
its widest point, and consists of an area of 1,754 square
miles, with a total acreage estimated at 1,195,500, of
which 312,000 are returned as under cultivation.

About 570,000 were held by the Government, up to
the advent of the oil industry, the remaining portion,
approximating some 500,000 acres, being held by out-
siders and local syndicates.

The colony was taken from Spain in the year 1797,
by an expedition under Sir Ralph Abercromby, and has
continued as a British possession up to this day.

In 1909 the population of Trinidad numbered about
350,000, including coolie immigrants.

The government is administered by an executive
council and a nominated legislature, members holding
their seats for five years.

With the exception of India, Trinidad stands out boldly

as one of the most striking examples of British autocracy.

In this colony the taxpayers have no voice in the choosing of the people who are supposed to represent them in the Legislature, and it is doubtful whether this "august body" ever sought to protect the interest of the ratepayers where their own is not directly or indirectly at stake.

The chief seaport and city is Port of Spain, with a population estimated at 55,000, about one-third of which are East Indian coolies, and some remnant of that part of feudal France which emigrated during the religious troubles in that country to the West Indies.

Unlike other British West Indian towns, there is a total absence of the middle-man in the commercial life of Port of Spain.

The business is carried on through large department stores, in which one can purchase from a pin to an anchor —they cater for the needs of the classes and the masses.

No business place in the city of Port of Spain, except saloons (and by the by these are all practically owned by one family) makes any attempt to specialize or, in other words, to deal in any one line of merchandise. The principle seems to be to get as many departments as possible under one roof.

Native cabinet-making has taken long strides in this colony, though it is still very much below perfection.

The weak points appear to be in the lack of special knowledge of treating the different grades of wood used in the manufacture of these articles, and in the finishing.

In these particulars they do not come up to the imported furniture, class for class.

The one encouraging thing about this industry is that most of the large stores carry an almost exclusive stock of native-made furniture, which is an example most worthy of copy by West Indian merchants in other colonies.

Harbour improvements in Trinidad are yet in their infancy. There are no wharves to admit large vessels alongside. Large vessels are obliged to anchor some three or four miles off shore, and the sea along the waterfront is filled with mud, emitting a very offensive odour when disturbed.

The only political organization in this island is the Working Men's Association, which, while looking out for the interest of the working men locally, embraces a much wider area.

The association is affiliated with the Labour Party in England, and is incorporated under the laws of the colony.

The method of working the organization is to have annual meetings, at which a committee is selected to handle all questions of interest, affecting the society or bearing on the colony's welfare, without having recourse to public meetings.

By this means they manage to fight from under cover where the attacked is unable to see the attacking force —a sort of " Spion Kop " business.

Mr. Alfred Richards, the president of the Association, is the only visible target, but he is by far not the most influential member—indeed, its followers are to be found even in the inner circles of the most exclusive set.

I had the pleasure of being an honoured guest at one of their secret meetings, and was astonished to note the amount of talent present.

They were most of them from the educated class, with some working men of undoubted ability. The majority of those whom I saw were young men of determined demeanour, who have evidently set themselves to accomplish a purpose.

The chief products of the colony are pitch, manjack, cocoa, coco-nuts, bananas, sugar, rum, and *petroleum*.

Government.—Autocratic.

BARBADOS

" Little England, " as the garden island of West Indies is popularly called, reminds one of a well-kept tennis court.

Everywhere is tidiness itself. This colony fell into the hands of the English during the reign of James I., in the year 1605, where it has remained to this day.

It was discovered by Columbus at about the same period that Jamaica was annexed to the Spanish flag.

Bridgetown, the capital of this little island, is a most compact city and was founded in 1628 by Wolferstone, a native of Bermuda, acting under orders of the Earl of Carlisle, after whom Carlisle Bay, Barbados, is named.

There is no coolie immigration to Barbados. The cultivation of sugar, cotton, etc., is carried on with native labour, thus giving the contradiction to the statements that the negroes of the West Indies dislike working on the estates and that they are shiftless, lazy, and always ready for a song.

There is an over-abundance of skilled and intelligent labour in the colony. The surplus of these are willing to seek homes in the less crowded sister colonies, but their free immigration is hampered by legislative restrictions. They are disliked as field-labourers from the fact of their intelligence, and West Indian planters do not care to employ them on that score.

The colonial immigrant must be able to show a certain

amount of money before he is permitted to land in a sister colony, where a livelihood can be got, though he is starving in his own.

Until we have a confederation (a political and commercial union) of these colonies, with their present divergent sentiments, under *responsible government*, these evils, which show every tendency to increase, will continue indefinitely.

These petty restrictions are, to say the least, a detriment to the development of these colonies.

The population of Barbados is estimated at 200,000, all thrifty, hardworking, and industrious.

At present nine different lines of steamships call at Bridgetown on their way out from Europe, thus supporting my plea as to its suitability as one of the great depositing and distributing stations of the confederacy.

The constitution of Barbados comes nearer what we should all have, than that of any of the other West Indian colonies.

The government is a representative one for all practical purposes.

The Barbadians refused to be hoodwinked in abandoning freedom for that mild form of slavery, which was so ingenuously proposed to the West Indies when they were being stripped of their franchise.

They absolutely refused, under coercion from the Home Government, to exchange the reality for the shadow; they refused to say: "We are unfit to manage our own affairs."

Hence it is that "Little England" is to-day the envy of her sister colonies, for she alone among them has the right to say: "I will," or "I will not."

The islanders run the "show" and they run it well,

even though the Imperial Government reserves the right to appoint and control certain public offices.

Sugar is the chief article of export. There are upwards of 64,000 acres under cane-cultivation, and as late as 1908 there were about 400 sugar works in operation.

The total yield in 1902 was 52,000 hogsheads of sugar and 42,000 puncheons of molasses.

There is possibly no part in the West Indies where cotton is so largely grown as in this island. In 1907 the total value of this product exported to the United Kingdom reached the handsome figure of eighty-two thousand pounds sterling.

Government.—Representative (?).

BRITISH GUIANA

This beautiful, large, and fertile colony is to be found on the mainland of South America.

It is bounded on the south by Brazil, and on the west by Venezuela, but was never a possession of either country.

The capital, Georgetown, has a population of 54,000, of which nearly one-half is made up of East Indians and their descendants.

The country extends from east to west for about 300 miles and about 500 from north to south, and consists of a total area of 90,000 square miles. Of this amount only 130 square miles are returned as under cultivation, which is the net result of British occupation extending over a century.

British Guiana was first settled by the Dutch in 1621. During the wars of the French Revolution it was captured by the British, but in 1796 it was again restored to Dutch control, only to be retaken by the English a year later, to whom, in 1814, it was finally ceded.

Quite within the recollection of the present generation there occurred a dispute between Venezuela and Britain, over the boundary along the western border of this magnificent province, which nearly precipitated into an armed conflict between the United States of America and Great Britain. Everyone will remember that famous message which Cleveland sent to the U.S. Congress in 1895 which was tantamount to a declaration of war.

Had England but raised a finger against Venezuela after this act on the part of the United States, a grave crisis would have been precipitated.

It was no Yankee bluff, either; every word of that message was meant, and was backed up by the army and navy of the United States.

Every ship in the navy upon which a gun could be mounted was secretly ordered into commission; officers on furlough were ordered to report for duty; thousands of extra hammers tinkered away night and day, in her arsenals and dockyards all over the country—America was ready for war.

Then Great Britain yielded, and there was no war. It made the Yankees chuckle and laugh in their sleeve to see the *lion* curl up and wag its tail as a sign of defeat. England was caught napping—she was unprepared for war and consequently was forced to accept the dictation of the younger giant of the west.

Let us hope that the lesson taught her has been acted upon.

The dispute was finally referred to arbitration, and the award was to the effect—That the boundary as set out by Sir R. Schomburgh *was not a* good, natural boundary, and that Great Britain had exceeded her claims, and was therefore wrong in her contention.

The interest of Venezuela as a contending party was completely submerged by the United States, in the interest of the Monroe Doctrine.

It was an issue between England and America—a test of the *Monroe Doctrine*, and the Yankees were ready to show how far they were willing to go for its preservation.

Not since 1823, when President Monroe laid down this burdensome doctrine, was there ever such a test as to the seriousness of its purpose, and, notwithstanding that all South Americans are at some time or the other ready to repudiate its claim upon them, yet they very readily fall back under its ever-protecting wings and assume a demeanour of arrogance when threatened by an outside power.

The trouble over boundaries was not over, however, for very soon after Brazil, on the southern borders, sent up a dismal howl against British encroachment. Again the indefatigable Yankees were on the alert, scenting for trouble.

There was to be no trouble. Negotiations for the settlement of the difficulty were soon begun and proceeded rapidly.

In 1901 a treaty was concluded for the arbitration of the dispute.

The King of Italy, who was agreed upon as the arbitrator, gave his decision two years later to the effect :—That Great Britain had claimed twice as much territory from Brazil as she was entitled to. Again the " lion " was forced to beat a retreat before the onslaught of the Monroe Doctrine. It was an unmistakable sign that a new champion had arisen in the West, and Europe took the hint.

What would have been the effect of Britain's demands on the territory of her two neighbours, had not providence in all her wisdom furnished this wonderful doctrine, and a still more wonderful nation to enforce it, can be readily surmised.

At one time the staple products of this colony consisted of many articles of commerce, but for some reason they have all, one by one, been forced to give way to the cultivation of cane.

There are forty-three estates (sugar) in British Guiana, covering a total of 159,000 acres, of which only 72,000, or about one-half, are under cultivation, the uncultivated portions being in the category of hoarded lands.

Quite recently the cultivation of cocoa and rice has taken enormous strides in the colony—of the latter industry (rice) fully 30,000 acres are under cultivation.

In 1907–8 gold to the extent of £239,000, and diamonds value £3,000, were exported.

Government.—Autocratic.

THE WINDWARD ISLANDS

This group consists of St. Lucia, St. Vincent, Grenada, and a still smaller group known as the Grenadines, lying between the last two islands.

ST. LUCIA

This island was discovered by Columbus in 1502, about eight years after he touched at Jamaica—that was on his fourth voyage to the West Indies.

It is 24 miles long and 12 wide, containing about 233 square miles.

The towns of greatest importance are Castries and

Soufrière, the former with 5,000 inhabitants, and the latter between 2,500 and 3,000.

St. Lucia was a French possession from 1642 to 1793. During that time it was attacked by an expedition led by one " Thomas Warner, a bastard son of the governor of St. Christopher," but the French soon drove the invaders from the island.

In the year 1794 the island was captured by the British, but was surrendered to the French in 1802, only to be re-taken a few months later (war having broken out afresh between the two powers), and it has remained in British hands ever since.

The total population of the island is estimated at 54,000. Of these about 5 per cent. are white.

The official language of the colony is English—though most of the people prefer to speak the *patois* (corrupt French).

The majority of these people are far from being reconciled with the " English " ; they prefer to be known as French, and speak of the negroes of the other British West Indian colonies as *neg Anglais*, as distinct from *neg Français*—thus claiming a sort of superiority for everything French.

From the fact that Government lands can be obtained at one pound sterling per acre, payable in instalments, and the soil will grow all kinds of tropical produce, it is most surprising that the island is not in a prosperous condition.

The secret of this stagnation seems to lie in the lack of proper governmental assistance, and this is mainly so throughout the entire British West Indies.

Agricultural banks, the platform of every agricultural conference, imperial or otherwise, in these colonies for the past years, should be established throughout the possessions, with as little delay as possible, and thus give relief to this state of chronic stagnation.

Government.—Autocratic.

ST. VINCENT

This island, also one of the many discoveries of Columbus, is 18 miles long, 11 broad, and comprises about 85,000 square miles.

It is about a hundred miles from Barbados, and twenty-one miles from St. Lucia.

Here is to be seen the " Soufrière," a volcanic mountain, which for a long period was supposed to be extinct, as it had given no evidence of life since its eruption in 1812.

It was not until 1902, fully ninety years after, when Mt. Pelee broke loose in Martinique, that this seemingly peaceful, slumbering mountain, one of the most striking natural features of the island, belched forth torrents of hot sand and a river of boiling lava which completely devastated the northern part of the island.

Fully two thousand of the inhabitants lost their lives in this catastrophe, and thousands were rendered homeless.

Among the products of the colony are arrowroot, starch, rum, sugar, and cotton.

St. Vincent has had its share of French tutelage during the early period.

In 1796, Sir Ralph Abercromby subdued the combined French and Carib opposition, firmly establishing British mastery over the colony.

The emancipation of the slaves followed in 1838, after which Portuguese and coolie labourers were introduced.

Kingstown is the chief seaport of the island and contains about 52,000 inhabitants.

Government.—Autocratic.

GRENADA

The Island of Grenada is 21 miles long, 12 broad, and contains about 133 square miles.

St. George is the principal town, with about 5,000 inhabitants. It has the reputation of being a very healthy colony, possessing a fine harbour and an abundant supply of the purest kind of water.

There are numerous mineral springs throughout the island.

The total population is set down at 71,000, of which only 2 per cent. are white.

Grenada is a comparatively flourishing country, which is due to the abundance of peasant proprietary who did not confine themselves to the planting of sugar-cane alone. Hence, when king sugar was killed by the free-trade giant, the island suffered only to a minor extent compared to those colonies whose salvation and sole reliance rested upon the mercies of large estates held by corporations.

Sugar-cane culture is almost extinct in the island, and consequently there is no importation of coolie labour.

The 3,000 East Indians now in the colony are the only traces left of a long-defunct traffic in human beings.

Like most of the Lesser Antilles, Grenada was once inhabited by the French, who founded in the year 1650 the present town of St. George. Columbus discovered this island in 1498 and called it " Concepcion."

The constitution of the colony at the beginning of the British regime provided for an upper and lower house, but in 1875 a single house was established in lieu, and a semi-pronounced system of Crown Colony Government inaugurated.

Following the usual course of things, the assembly

one year after (1876), is credited to have drafted a petition to the Home Government, praying for its own extinction and the matter of providing a suitable form of administration was left to the wisdom of Her Majesty's Government.

The result was—the inauguration of a purely nominated system.

In 1885 Grenada became the headquarters for St. Vincent and St. Lucia.

The chief product is cocoa, which yields an annual revenue of over £250,000 ; but coffee, nutmeg, spices, and cotton are also grown.

Government.—Autocratic.

THE LEEWARD ISLANDS

The population of the Leeward Islands is estimated at 129,250, scattered over an area of 704 square miles.

They are Antigua, St. Christopher (St. Kitt's), Nevis, Dominica, and Montserrat, Anguilla, etc.

During the early periods each of these islands enjoyed some form of representative government.

In the year 1871 the Imperial Parliament passed an Act constituting these islands into a single colony.

These islands have been in the possession of Great Britain for over a century, but appear to be retrograding instead of advancing.

Much might be written in a way, about each individual plane, but space will not now permit.

It suffices to say that their only salvation lay in a larger scheme for a general confederation with responsible government.

Among their chief products are to be found sugar, cotton, pineapple, lime juice, oils, and spices.

Government.—Autocratic.

THE BAHAMAS

It would seem uncharitable, were I to close my remarks on the " West Indian Colonies," which would come under the federation, without saying a word on the *Bahamas*.

These are a chain of coral islands, about thirty-nine in number, of which only eighteen or twenty are inhabited.

The total area of these islands is estimated at 4,466 square miles, with a population of 60,000.

New Providence is the most important of them, and here is where the capital is situated.

This town has been for a long time a favourite watering-place for the better class of Americans, who flock there to escape the rigours of the North American winters.

Here, as in Jamaica, we find American influence in combat with English influence and manner, showing a decided gain for the Yankees.

Withdraw American support (patronage) from the Bahamas and the whole " chain " goes up in smoke, so dependent are they on the people and markets of the United States.

The Bahamas, after a series of alternate invasions by British and Spaniards, were finally ceded to Great Britain in 1786, in whose hands they have been allowed to rest.

The trade is chiefly with the United States and its industries are for the most part financed by American capitalists. The islands are only British by name ; still they are possessed with a sort of reckless loyalty, which will be hard to eradicate.

One of the most important articles of export is sisal hemp, which in 1907 fetched the respectable sum of £47,000.

Sponge fishing is, however, the most remunerative

item of export at present. The amount realized for this article in the same year (1907) was £130,000.

Citron, fruit, pineapples, and preserved fruits, each add their quota to the resources of the islands.

Strange, too, that in the early history of North America, when there was such a thing as a *royalist* in what is now the United States of America, large amounts of cotton were grown and exported from the Bahamas, but for some unexplainable reason the industry has been allowed to die a natural death.

Let us hope that the day is not far distant when cultivation of cotton will again take its place as the chief item of export of this magnificent " chain of coral islands."

Government.—Representative.

THE END